P9-CCY-851

# Marty Mann Answers Your Questions About Drinking and Alcoholism

# Marty Mann Answers Your Questions About Drinking and Alcoholism



Holt, Rinehart and Winston
New York

Published by Holt, Rinehart and Winston,
383 Madison Avenue, New York, New York 10017.

Published simultaneously in Canada by Holt, Rinehart and Winston of Canada, Limited.

Library of Congress Cataloging in Publication Data

Mann, Marty, 1904–
Marty Mann answers your questions about drinking and alcoholism.

Bibliography: p.
1. Alcoholism—Miscellanea. II. Alcoholism—United States Miscellanea. 3. Liquor problem—United States—Miscellanea. I. Title.
HV5035.M35 1981 616.86′1 80-28349

ISBN Hardbound: 0-03-081857-5
ISBN Paperback: 0-03-059156-2

First published in hardcover by Holt, Rinehart and Winston in 1970.

First Owl Book Edition—1981

Printed in the United States of America
10 9 8 7 6 5 4 3 2 1

To
Chris, Betty, and Bill Mann
with love

# Contents


| | | |
|---|---|---|
| | Preface | ix |
| 1. | Facts and Figures | 1 |
| 2. | Myths and Misconceptions | 11 |
| 3. | Drinking | 20 |
| 4. | Alcoholism | 29 |
| 5. | Recognition | 39 |
| 6. | Symptoms | 47 |
| 7. | The Alcoholic | 56 |
| 8. | The Woman Alcoholic | 62 |
| 9. | Causes | 67 |
| 10. | Denial or the Alibi System | 73 |
| 11. | Approaches to the Alcoholic | 80 |
| 12. | Treatment | 87 |
| 13. | Alcoholics Anonymous | 95 |
| 14. | Al-Anon and Alateen | 106 |
| | Bibliography | 111 |

# Preface

Thirty years of experience in the midst of this fascinating, devastating, and often baffling problem of alcoholism have convinced me of the great need for a book which answers, as simply and directly as possible, some of the myriad questions people ask. For people do ask, anyone who they think may have some answers, at every opportunity and on every occasion. Those who are in any way associated with alcoholism, however remotely, have had such experiences hundreds of times. At social gatherings for instance, such knowledgeable ones may have no opportunity to break away, or to talk about anything else, so insistent are the questioners. Even at business, professional, or other meetings, when it becomes known that an individual has some connection with these matters he becomes a target for questions.

The questions range far and wide: sometimes simple and basic, other times complex and involved. Many of them could be called universal in that almost everyone asks them. Many others have answers widely enough known so that we in the field are apt to make the mistake of assuming that everyone knows at least this much.

It is clear that everyone does not. It is equally clear that almost everyone wants to know at least some of these things, to have some of the knowledge that is presently available about drinking, and most particularly about problem drinking or alcoholism.

It is said that knowledge brings power. In this case, knowledge could well bring health, happiness, and a productive life to millions of people. My own life is a case in point. For five terrible years I struggled to *regain* my drinking equilibrium, with no knowledge whatsoever that this was impossible for me, or of why it was impossible. I knew nothing of alcoholism, of what it was or what could be done about it. And none of the doctors whose help I sought in those horrible years seemed to know. I thought I had lost my mind, a thought that struck such terror in me that that loss seemed even greater than the other losses I was suffering. Yet these last included everything I valued or cared for, since with alcoholism one loses everything, bit by bit, but inevitably. Unless one finds help and recovers as, at long last, I did.

My own recovery began in 1939, and five years later I had reached the conclusion that some vast and special effort was needed to bring the kind of knowledge that had saved my life, to everyone. Scientific backing was necessary if this information, so contrary to the thinking prevalent at that time, was to gain public acceptance. That backing was forthcoming from a remarkable group of pioneers—a handful of scientists then working on this problem at Yale University. With their encouragement and support, the National Council on Alcoholism (NCA) was founded in 1944.

NCA's major purpose, as indicated in its original name,

National Committee for Education on Alcoholism, was to teach the public the facts about alcoholism and what could be done about it, hoping to change public attitudes from negative apathy to positive action, to eradicate the stigma which for so long had held alcoholism and its victims captive in the deep secrecy of shame, and to initiate community action programs which would carry on education and fight for more and better facilities for care and treatment.

As Executive Director and chief spokesman for the fledgling organization, I stumped the country talking before any and every group that offered me a hearing, always basing my talks on NCA's three concepts:

1. Alcoholism is a disease and the alcoholic a sick person.
2. The alcoholic can be helped and is worth helping.
3. This is a public health problem and therefore a public responsibility.

Those were dark days. Medical care was usually not available. Treatment facilities were almost nonexistent. But there *was* Alcoholics Anonymous, present in almost every community, eager and willing to help if the alcoholic would let them, and showing a high rate of recovery for those who would give it a chance. There was hope. And hope was the message I carried, hope and a call to action.

Thousands of citizens, both lay and professional, heeded that call. Action programs have spread throughout the country. Yet the spread of knowledge and of the hope contained in that knowledge has still not been fast enough or far-reaching enough to bring more than a fraction of those in need to the help that is now available. As in other health areas there is a death-dealing gap between the knowledge we have and its full use. It is my hope that this book will help to close that gap by bringing to the public some of the valid information about drinking and alcoholism that is so urgently needed.

*New York, New York* *Marty Mann*
*June, 1969*

# Imagine Such a Disease

If some new and terrible disease were suddenly to strike us here in America—a disease of unknown cause, possibly due to noxious gas or poison in our soil, air, or water—it would be treated as a national emergency, with our whole citizenry uniting as a man to fight it.

Let us suppose the disease to have so harmful an effect on the nervous system that 10 million people in our country would go insane for periods lasting from a few hours to weeks or months and recurring repetitively over periods ranging from 15 to 30 years.

Let us further suppose that during these spells of insanity, acts of so destructive a nature would be committed that the material and spiritual lives of whole families would be in jeopardy, with a resultant 40 million persons cruelly affected. Work in business, industry, professions, and factories would be crippled, sabotaged, or left undone. And each year more than one and one-quarter billion dollars would need to be spent merely to patch up in some small way the effects of the disease on families whose breadwinners have been stricken.

Finally, let us imagine this poison or disease to have the

peculiar property of so altering a person's judgment, so brainwashing him that he would be unable to see that he had become ill at all; actually so perverting and so distorting his view of life that he would wish with all his might to go on being ill.

Such an emergency would unquestionably be classed as a countrywide disaster, and billions of dollars and thousands of scientists would be put to work to find the cause of the disease, to treat its victims, and to prevent its spread.

The dread disease envisioned above is actually here. It is alcoholism.

Ruth Fox, M.D.
*President, American Medical Society on Alcoholism*

# Marty Mann Answers Your Questions About Drinking and Alcoholism

# 1. Facts and Figures

**Q. Most Americans drink, don't they?**

**A.** Yes. Drinking is an accepted social custom in our society and a majority of our adult population drinks —about 70 per cent.

**Q. What about the 30 per cent who don't drink?**

**A.** They are abstainers, mostly for religious reasons, some for health reasons, and some because they just don't like it. Then of course there are recovered alcoholics, perhaps half a million people, who cannot drink because of their alcoholism.

**Q. How many people does 70 per cent who drink, mean?**

**A.** Approximately 154,000,000 men and women.

**Q. Does that number include all kinds of drinkers?**

**A.** Yes, all the way from daily drinkers to those who drink only a few times a year, on special occasions.

**Q. How many are alcoholics?**

**A.** The count varies tremendously. Estimates of the number of alcoholics range from 9.3 to 10 million. And estimates of the proportion of drinkers who develop alcoholism range from 6 per cent to 10 per cent. The range can be so wide because there is no accurate count. Alcoholism has been hidden and denied for so long that no one really knows how many people are suffering from it. This situation is not unique: no one really knows how many Americans have heart disease or diabetes or even cancer, since many people have these conditions without knowing it or without its being reported. Alcoholism has an extra hazard since the stigma surrounding it leads to concealment of the condition, not only by the alcoholic but also by families, friends, co-workers, and employers. And all too often the condition is not recognized even by those close to the sufferer, who himself goes to great lengths to conceal it.

**Q. Who makes these estimates?**

**A.** There is no one single source. Scientists, doctors, medical and scientific journals and organizations, have all published figures. A publication of the American Medical Association carried the statement that 10 per cent of those who drink develop alcoholism. The estimates that have the widest acceptance are based on the Jellinek Formula, a mathematical projection using deaths from cirrhosis of the liver as a base. The late Dr. E. M. Jellinek was recognized as the world's greatest authority on the subject. He was the first Director of the Yale Center of Alcohol Studies, first Editor of the *Quarterly Journal of Studies on Alcohol,* Consultant on Alcoholism to the World Health Organization, and author of many scientific papers and of the authoritative book *The Disease Concept of Alcoholism.* A biostatistician, he developed the Jellinek Formula in 1943, estimating at that time some 3 million alcoholics in the United States. The *Quarterly Journal,* using figures from the Bureau of Vital Statistics for 1956, then revised the 3 million to 5 million. In 1965 the National Council on Alcoholism, using a projection of these Jellinek Formula figures, gave an estimate of 6.5 million. The United States Government, in a 1978 report of 1975 statistics, estimated 9.3 to 10 million alcoholics and problem drinkers.

**Q. Does this mean that alcoholism is increasing?**

**A.** In the number of people afflicted, yes. But apparently not in incidence per hundred thousand. Two factors largely account for the big jump: the increase in population, and the increase in percentage of those who drink, from 60 per cent in 1943 to 70 per cent in 1965.

**Q. Then alcoholism is a big problem?**

**A.** A past Secretary of Health, Education, and Welfare, Dr. Arthur Flemming, publicly named it our fourth major health problem, ranking with heart disease, cancer, and mental illness.

**Q. How serious is this problem?**

**A.** In numbers of people adversely affected it is our most serious public health problem since each alcoholic's illness affects at least four other persons—his immediate family. This means 40 million more than the 10 million alcoholics, a total of 50 million Americans, are directly and unfavorably affected by alcoholism. It is a serious problem to every one of us in another, frightening way: the Moynihan Report prepared for HEW's Committee on Traffic Safety states that 10 per cent of the nation's drivers are alcoholics, and recent studies show that more than 50 per cent of our fatal traffic accidents are alcohol-related. To all of us too it is a serious economic problem: in police court and jail costs, in welfare costs, in emergency and hospital costs in our city and county hospitals, and in a variety of other costs that are met by our tax dollars. Industry bears astronomical losses because of employees with unrecognized alcoholism—in 1975 an estimated $19.64 billion lost in production alone. And tragically, alcoholism ranks second as a cause of suicide in the United States. Depression is first. The seriousness of the illness to an alcoholic is simply stated: unless he seeks help, and the progression of the disease is stopped, he faces insanity or early death.

**Q. Is it a fact that alcoholism is a disease?**

**A.** The American Medical Association officially declared alcoholism a disease and a medical responsibility in 1956. Long before that time many doctors and medical groups had so stated, beginning with Dr. Thomas Trotter in 1778. Dr. Trotter took alcoholism as the subject for his dissertation (then necessary to get a medical degree) at the University of Edinburgh, was asked to expand it into a book, and on publication of his book in 1782 was awarded a gold medal by the British Humanitarian Society for his services to humanity. In this country the "father of American medicine," Dr. Benjamin Rush, published a book on alcoholism in 1802, labeling it a "vicious disease," the same phrase that Dr. Trotter had used. Today doctors working in the field, or who treat alcoholics, speak and write with near-unanimity of the disease of alcoholism, many specifying that it is a "disease entity."

**Q. Do people die of alcoholism?**

**A.** Yes. In the acute stage of the illness, for lack of medical care; by suicide, as mentioned above; from delirium tremens; from cirrhosis of the liver; from heart failure, and from many other physical complications of long-time excessive drinking. The 1978 United States Government report stated that in 1975, 205,000 deaths were alcohol-related, but this may be an understatement because of the stigma which still leads many kindly intentioned doctors to list only a secondary cause in order to spare the family's feelings. Consider the similarity to cancer, which was long stigmatized and for which obituaries still routinely use the euphemism "died after a long illness."

**Q. Does alcoholism really cause heart failure?**

**A.** Recent research indicates that it causes many unexplained deaths which are usually medically labeled "heart failure." The research findings are that even reasonable amounts of drinking can affect the heart enough so that when stress is added—tennis, shoveling snow, etc.—deaths from heart failure can result.

**Q. Is alcoholism hereditary?**

**A.** There have not been enough studies to prove this one way or the other. But empirical observations of many doctors who have checked their patients' family backgrounds indicate that at least a tendency to alcoholism exists in some families.

**Q. How about alcoholism and accidents?**

**A.** Studies have shown that alcoholics are seven times more likely than nonalcoholics to meet with fatal accidents, and four and a half times more likely to die in automobile accidents than nonalcoholics. Other studies indicate that 25 per cent of the accidental deaths caused by falling asleep with a lighted cigarette, cigar, or pipe are caused by the heavy use of alcohol, and that 25,000 deaths and 800,000 crashes due to drinking drivers or pedestrians occur in the United States each year.

**Q. Aren't most alcoholics unemployed?**

**A.** No, they are not. At least 6 million alcoholics are currently employed, giving industry one of its biggest headaches. An HEW study states that at least 70 per cent of all alcoholics are still on the job and have been there for fifteen to twenty-five years or more.

**Q. Is industry doing anything about this?**

**A.** After a slow start, industry, and the Government as an employer too, are becoming increasingly active in this field. A 1979 survey of the top 750 corporations in the United States showed that 56.7% had alcoholism programs for their employees. The number of smaller companies having constructive alcoholism policies and some kind of program is much larger.

**Q. What success are they having?**

**A.** Their rate of recovery is higher than that in a mixed group of people attending an alcoholism clinic or other treatment facility, ranging from 50 per cent to as high as 80 per cent, with a large number reporting 65 to 70 per cent.

**Q. Why should their rate be higher?**

**A.** First, this is a highly selected group, the majority of whom are long-time employees: fifteen to twenty-five years, as mentioned above, with good work records until their alcoholism intervened. Second, the situation provides motivation at a much earlier stage, since good industrial programs are built around early detection techniques. And finally, the motivating lever is strong—possible loss of job. After all, a man's job is his most important possession: without it he can't keep his family or anything else. The threat of this loss will move him to action more quickly and surely than any other method.

**Q. What constitutes recovery?**

**A.** In industry the criteria are a return to efficient functioning on the job, increased productivity, and good working relationships. This requires an interruption of the destructive drinking, preferably no drinking at all. But total abstinence is not industry's criterion; it is solely concerned with job performance. Nevertheless, most alcoholics who have recovered with the help of their company's alcoholism programs have accepted the fact that it is not safe for them to drink, and great numbers of them have joined Alcoholics Anonymous, which makes complete abstention from drinking the core of its recovery program.

**Q. Are there any organizations dealing with this problem?**

**A.** Yes. There are quite a number dealing with special aspects of alcoholism and alcohol problems, but the major one is the National Council on Alcoholism (NCA), the voluntary citizen-based organization with local affiliates throughout the country. Alcoholics Anonymous calls itself a fellowship rather than an organization, and the American Medical Society on Alcoholism is a professional association of doctors only, while the North Conway Institute directs its efforts to clergymen and church bodies. The Rutgers (formerly Yale) Center of Alcohol Studies is primarily concerned with research, runs Summer Institutes of Alcohol Studies for special and professional groups, and publishes the *Quarterly Journal of Studies on Alcohol* as well as other technical and scientific materials.

**Q. What is the Government doing?**

**A.** At the state level, government has been active in this field since the first well-funded tax-supported program was established in Connecticut in 1945. Today, every state in the nation has an alcoholism program. At the Federal level, activity really began in 1966 with the establishment, by Presidential directive, of the National Center for Prevention and Control of Alcoholism, and the National Advisory Committee on Alcoholism, to advise the Secretary of HEW on long-range planning and current activities. Congress too has become increasingly aware and interested, and it seems certain that good legislation will be passed and funded in the near future.

# 2. Myths and Misconceptions

**Q. Is there something wrong with people who don't drink?**

**A.** No. Drinking or not drinking is an intensely personal matter, and there are many, many reasons why some people don't do it. Apart from religious strictures or doctors' orders, there is an endless variety of reasons that may be overriding to the individual: he may loathe the taste or the effect, he may have seen someone he loved die of it, he may have had an unfortunate experience with drinking, or he may simply have decided that he valued his alertness and clear state of consciousness more than the temporary euphoria given by drinking.

**Q. Does nondrinking mean that someone is unlikable, or peculiar, or a stuffed shirt, or a blue-nose?**

**A.** Not necessarily, although some nondrinkers—and some drinkers too—may be any or all of these things. Many nondrinkers are warm, outgoing, likable, gregarious people with a good sense of humor, just as many drinkers are. The only "peculiar" thing about them is that they prefer ginger ale or tonic water to whiskey or gin.

**Q. Does drinking make people more attractive?**

**A.** Occasionally it may, if a normally tense, rigid, and nervous person becomes relaxed and comfortable with a drink or two. Such a person may be in danger, however, of becoming dependent on alcohol, the shadowy entry to the road called alcoholism. By and large, drinking doesn't really make people more *attractive*, it just makes them more evident: their tongues are loosed, their voices rise, their inhibitions are lowered, and there you are at a cocktail party, unable to hear yourself think.

**Q. Is an ability to drink more than other people a sign of virility?**

**A.** No, but it is likely to be an early symptom of alcoholism. Most alcoholics had the capacity to drink more than their friends (and that's an abnormal reaction to alcohol) when they started drinking. This was considered something to be proud of, so they always *did* drink more than anyone else—and their troubles may have started right there.

**Q. Is the old Latin proverb "*in vino veritas*" (literally, "in wine is truth") correct?**

**A.** Not for alcoholics, for in them drinking produces a personality change, and they tend to speak and to behave quite differently from their real selves. But in normal drinkers a few drinks may well bring out what they really think or feel, due to the lowering of inhibitions.

**Q. Is alcohol an aphrodisiac?**

**A.** No. It is a sedative, and in sufficient quantities, an anesthetic. The reason people mistake it for an aphrodisiac is because of its inhibition-lowering effect. There are those who would never dare make a sexual move cold sober, but after a few drinks will do so quite freely. Actually, large quantities of alcohol are a sex-inhibitor and can render a man temporarily impotent. For alcoholics far along in the progression of their disease this can last for a long time, continuing as long as they are drinking, and often for many months after they have stopped drinking. If they remain abstinent, however, the condition usually clears up. The myth that women alcoholics are inevitably sexually promiscuous is just that—a myth. In the first place, alcoholics, men and women, are not too interested in sex, except in a superficial way. Their interest is focused primarily on drinking. In the second place, a drunken woman is far from attractive and in most cases therefore, is not likely to be in too great danger.

**Q. Will switching drinks keep you from getting drunk?**

**A.** No. It's the alcohol that causes drunkenness, whether it's in wine, beer, whiskey, gin, or whatever.

**Q. They say "two beers never hurt anyone." Is this true?**

**A.** It depends what you mean by "hurt." Small amounts of liquor don't do any physical damage, but even small amounts—two beers, two whiskeys, two martinis—can slow the body's reaction time a measurable amount—just enough to make the difference in meeting a sudden emergency while driving, for example. Even more important is the fact that the same small amount of alcohol affects the judgment so that one *thinks* one is driving better than usual, whereas the opposite is true. This also can be a major factor in an emergency situation.

**Q. Does drinking help meet a difficult situation?**

**A.** It looks that way, since one or two drinks make a person *feel* more at ease and more courageous. But if alertness and judgment are needed, then the drinks may make the person less able to handle the difficult situation to his own satisfaction or benefit.

**Q. Does drinking help creativity?**

**A.** Alcohol releases inhibitions, so that small amounts may help some people overcome blocks caused by inhibition. However, since even small amounts affect judgment, the results may not be as good as the drinker thinks. Work done with the aid of drinks had better be reevaluated in the cold light of a sober morning.

**Q. Is drinking essential in certain occupations?**

**A.** Drinking is never *essential.* Any occupation can be carried on, and very well too, by a nondrinker if he has the occupational abilities needed for that job. It is true that certain occupations call for drinking by custom, but thousands of nondrinkers have shown themselves extremely capable of handling these very jobs. They simply order nonalcoholic drinks on drinking occasions, and they do not make a fuss about it. A Horse's Neck is a good drink to order because it is not readily recognizable for its nonalcoholic content (a plain ginger ale with a twist of lemon peel), and it looks like a Scotch and soda. No one is conspicuous drinking this.

**Q. Is drinking essential in certain social situations?**

**A.** Again, it is never essential. But a nondrinker can be made to feel very uncomfortable in some situations. Unfortunately there are too many ill-mannered hosts and hostesses who press drinks on their guests, even after a polite refusal. The manner in which the guest refuses has much to do with putting a stop to this. It is necessary to be very, very firm, and sometimes to go as far as saying, "Sorry, but I don't drink." If you are a nondrinker it may be pleasanter for you simply to avoid such situations and the people who create them. If you cannot, then work out your own technique of refusing. It can be done.

**Q. Is someone who drinks every day an alcoholic?**

**A.** No. There are many moderate drinkers who have a few drinks every day. There are heavy drinkers who are daily drinkers too, but this does not mean they have alcoholism.

**Q. If someone gets drunk every weekend is he an alcoholic?**

**A.** Probably not, if he does not get drunk during the week. Alcoholics generally cannot limit the times they get drunk to specified days and places.

**Q. Is alcoholism hopeless?**

**A.** The old phrase "hopeless drunk" is pure myth. This is one of those two-words-used-as-one (like damyankee) that is deeply imbedded in the language, signifying widespread belief in it. The "hopeless" has been blasted from the double word by the hundreds of thousands of alcoholics who have recovered in the past thirty years, through A.A. and other means. It is now believed that there is no such thing as a "hopeless drunk," providing he can be got to treatment.

**Q. What is the biggest myth about alcoholism?**

**A.** That the Skid Row derelict is *the* alcoholic, and if someone has a job, a home, and a family, he can't be one. This comforting belief means to most of those who hold it, that "it can't be me, or mine," since it is confined to Skid Row areas. Even doctors believe this myth and rarely diagnose their private patients as having alcoholism, despite the fact that many of them, as interns, served in emergency wards of big city hospitals where they routinely diagnosed alcoholism in the Skid Row and poverty-stricken men who were brought there. A common way of expressing this particular myth is, "Why *he* can't be an alcoholic, he belongs to my club!"

**Q. They say beer drinkers never become alcoholics. Is this true?**

**A.** Not entirely, although it is rare for someone who drinks only beer to develop alcoholism, it takes so much of it to get drunk. Nevertheless, there have been alcoholics who drank only beer, and in Germany most alcoholics are almost exclusively beer drinkers.

**Q. How about wine drinkers?**

**A.** Many wine drinkers develop alcoholism, but this does not apply to those who only drink wine with their meals. "Winos" drink fortified wine, which has spirits added to it, and this produces a particularly virulent kind of drunkenness, with berserk behavior. Even those alcoholics who drink only unadulterated wine seem to exhibit greater psychological ill effects than other alcoholics.

**Q. Are some occupations more conducive to alcoholism than others?**

**A.** Yes, in the sense that they make it easier to continuously consume very large quantities without appearing too "different." In certain occupations where by custom and general consent a lot of business is conducted over drinks, an individual's alcoholism can progress very much further before it becomes noticeable.

**Q. Are alcoholics weak-willed?**

**A.** No. This is the second biggest myth about alcoholism. Most alcoholics have more than their share of will power. They have usually accomplished a good deal in their lives before alcoholism caught up with them. They will get up and go to work when anyone else, feeling as they do, would be in bed calling for the doctor. With single-mindedness of purpose they will manage to find liquor when there simply isn't any way to get it—this would be called "an iron will" if it were directed toward anything but liquor. And it takes both determination and will to pursue the uphill road to recovery, by whatever method; yet thousands of alcoholics have successfully done so. It has even been said that it takes a strong will to be a practicing alcoholic: to force down those morning drinks (essential medicine) when everything in your body rebels against them at the same time that same body is screaming for their effect.

**Q. Can anyone become an alcoholic?**

**A.** At our present stage of knowledge the answer would seem to be yes. Certainly any kind or type of person can and does develop alcoholism. There is no immunity conferred by background, position in life, money or the lack of it, by profession or occupation, or by sex.

# 3. Drinking

**Q. Why do people drink?**

**A.** There may be a thousand answers for a thousand individuals, but the one common denominator for them all is simply: *Because it makes them feel better.*

**Q. There must be other major reasons, aren't there?**

**A.** Yes, there are. Alcohol relieves tension, and many people use it for this purpose. It makes you forget your troubles—temporarily. It produces euphoria, makes you feel good, again temporarily. So people use it to escape, to relax, to have pleasure. Some people really like the taste, and drink for this reason. Others feel a social pressure to drink, and do it to conform. Still others are inhibited people who find it difficult to make small talk; drinking lowers their inhibitions and loosens their tongues, helps them to feel comfortable with other people. But in all these cases it makes them feel better than they did without the drinks.

**Q. Are there many kinds of drinking?**

**A.** Yes. But they can be coalesced under four major headings: occasional drinking, moderate drinking, heavy drinking, and alcoholic drinking.

**Q. What is meant by occasional drinking?**

**A.** Drinking only a few times a year, or only on special occasions such as weddings, christenings, or parties.

**Q. What is moderate drinking?**

**A.** This varies with the social customs of the individual, but in general it means never more than one or two drinks on any drinking occasion. A person might have one or two drinks every night before dinner, but rarely more than two, and still be a moderate drinker. Or he might limit his drinking to weekends and have very few drinks at any one time. Moderate drinking is really drinking small amounts.

**Q. Does moderate drinking do any harm?**

**A.** Research has shown that as little as two martinis a day for one month will produce signs of a fatty liver. But one month without a drink will reverse this situation. However even moderate drinking takes its toll: life expectancy is ten to twelve years less.

**Q. What about heavy drinking?**

**A.** In our society heavy drinking seems to be the norm—at least in urban and suburban areas. Many people have drinks with their lunch, suburban housewives often drink while playing bridge in the afternoons, the cocktail hour is sacred before dinner, and all these same people are likely to have several drinks after dinner. This adds up to quite a large consumption of alcohol, and while it may not be every day, it is often enough to put them way beyond moderate drinking. It is the amount consumed at any one time, plus the number of times a day or week that this occurs, that determines heavy drinking. A very large number of Americans are heavy drinkers.

**Q. Are heavy drinking and hard drinking the same thing?**

**A.** Not really. Heavy drinking means a large consumption every day or several times a week, but hard drinking means just that: going at it hard and steadily at any and all hours, often without showing drunkenness. Or drinking to saturation or near-drunkenness on every drinking occasion. Or perhaps to drunkenness on some occasions. By and large, hard drinking means constant drinking, during the day as well as night.

**Q. What is alcoholic drinking?**

**A.** It differs from all other kinds of drinking in a number of ways. The alcoholic drinks very fast—is always ready for a refill long before anyone else. The alcoholic gets all the drinks he can politely get, and then, if at all possible, sneaks a few extra. He gets drunker than anyone else, quicker than anyone else, even at a hard-drinking party. And even after a few drinks his personality changes: he often becomes argumentative, contentious, difficult, boisterous, or noisy. He is apt to stick out like a sore thumb in a group, behaving differently from the others, and apparently quite unaware of this.

**Q. What is the difference between heavy drinking and alcoholic drinking?**

**A.** The major difference is loss of control: the alcoholic consistently drinks more than he intended to, and gets drunk at the wrong time and place. But to the casual eye there is no difference in the earlier years of his drinking, because the differences are still largely within the drinker. However there are a few overt signs even then: gulping drinks, which leads to regularly drinking more than the rest of the group, with an ability not to show any signs of drunkenness; eagerness to serve as bartender at a party (he can sneak a few), many absences from the room, an obvious personality change after a few drinks. The difference was well described in ancient times by Seneca, the Roman writer (4 B.C. to 63 A.D.), in his *Epistolae Morales*: Posidonius maintains that the word "drunken" is used in two ways—in the one case of a man who is loaded with wine and has no control over himself; in the other of a man who is accustomed to get drunk, and is a slave to the habit. . . . You will surely admit that there is a great difference between a man who is drunk and a drunkard. He who is actually drunk may be in this state for the first time and may not have the habit, (and) the drunkard is often free from drunkenness.

**Q. What is normal drinking?**

**A.** So-called "normal" drinking varies enormously—from moderate to heavy—because it means simply the same kind of drinking as that of the others in your group, whatever that may be.

**Q. What is a social drinker?**

**A.** One who drinks the way his social group drinks, never overstepping their unwritten and unspoken, but very real bounds.

**Q. What does it mean if you have to have two or three drinks every night?**

**A.** It means you are dependent on those drinks, if you have to have them. And being dependent on alcohol is not a good thing, for it is out of the ranks of dependent drinkers that alcoholics emerge. Nevertheless, many people *like* having a few drinks every night, and this may not be dangerous at all. It is dependence that is dangerous.

**Q. Is it true that we are a hard-drinking country?**

**A.** Not today, although we apparently were in our frontier days. And at one period in our history, most men seem to have been hard drinkers. Dr. Jellinek (see Chapter 1, "Facts and Figures") had a word for it. He said that "during the late eighteenth and early nineteenth centuries users were boozers." Perhaps we could be called a heavy-drinking country, since most of our population lives in the urban and suburban areas, where this is almost a norm. Remember, however, that 30 per cent, or nearly one third, of our adult population doesn't drink at all.

**Q. Is our heavy drinking due to the particular stresses of our times?**

**A.** Not necessarily, considering what Dr. Jellinek said about earlier times. Others said similar things:

Thomas Jefferson, writing to a friend named Charles Yancey in 1815, said he intended to promote the sale of wine and beer "since whiskey is killing one third of our citizens." It was then believed that "ardent spirits" were the cause of the trouble and that wine and beer were safe drinks. Some Europeans still believe this and while strongly promoting the abolition of hard liquors, exempt wine and beer and drink both freely.

**Q. Has drinking always existed?**

**A.** Alcohol was discovered, probably through accidental fermentation, before writing was invented, and men promptly drank it and have been drinking it, in one form or another, ever since. Throughout history there have been efforts to outlaw it, none of which succeeded. One example was the decree of a Chinese emperor about 2000 B.C. that anyone who made, sold, distributed, or drank alcoholic beverages would be beheaded. This may have slowed things down a bit during his lifetime, but if it was like our own country under Prohibition, it only cranked things up!

**Q. Did people drink as much in times past as we do today?**

**A.** As much and more, in many different periods. During the decline of the Roman Empire, for instance, and during the Hundred Years' War in the area that is now Germany. Also during the eighteenth century in England, and in many other times and places. There seem always to have been periods of guzzling.

**Q. Why is drinking so important to people?**

**A.** For all those reasons why people drink, and more besides. In earliest times wine was equated with blood, and blood with life. Religious significance was given to wine, and still is in the Jewish faith. Perhaps a more important reason is a statement recently made by a doctor that liquor is such an effective tranquilizer that if it didn't exist we would have to invent it.

**Q. Then alcohol is very valuable?**

**A.** Again quoting medical opinions: had alcohol just been invented it would be considered the miracle drug of all ages. BUT . . . it probably would not be approved by the Food and Drug Administration, since recent research indicates it is one of the most toxic drugs we have.

**Q. Is there more drinking in the United States than in other countries?**

**A.** Statistics say no, for statistics give only per capita consumption, and several other countries have a higher per capita consumption than we do. France and Italy, for instance. But this doesn't take into account our 30 per cent who don't drink, nor does it take note of the ways of drinking in all three countries. Italians rarely drink without eating. The French sip away at wine and *aperitifs* all day long, and many French workers start their day with coffee and brandy. Americans, on the other hand, tend to bunch their drinking, mostly into the "cocktail hour" and again in the evening. This bunching may make it appear that there is more drinking here; or again because of the constricted hours when most drinking is done, Americans may drink more.

# 4.

# Alcoholism

**Q. What is alcoholism?**

**A.** It is a progressive disease, with identifiable and recognizable symptoms, which gradually makes people's drinking go out of control.

**Q. Who says it's a disease?**

**A.** Doctors who treat it, and it is doctors who decide what is a disease. Also the American Medical Association (see Chapter 1, "Facts and Figures"), the American Hospital Association, and the World Health Organization.

**Q. What do you mean by progressive?**

**A.** It moves inexorably from good to bad to worse (early to middle to late stages) over the years unless the alcoholic interrupts the progression by seeking help and getting treatment. Nothing can stop the progress except stopping the drinking.

**Q. If it's a disease, it can be cured, can't it?**

**A.** No, it cannot, it can only be arrested, just as in diabetes. A cure would mean that the alcoholic could drink normally, and this has happened so rarely that it is not considered a possible goal of treatment. It can be arrested only if the alcoholic stops drinking. And stays stopped. For good.

**Q. You mean he should never drink again?**

**A.** Exactly. It is not safe for an alcoholic to touch alcohol in any form, and this includes wine, beer, certain cough medicines and tonics, or anything else that contains alcohol even in small quantities. Even the smallest amount of alcohol can and sometimes does trigger the disease into becoming active again.

**Q. Why can't he stop by using his will power?**

**A.** He can't stop drinking by simply willing to stop any more than a tubercular can stop coughing by willing to stop. In both cases he may be able to stop for short periods, but these don't last unless he has the help and treatment he needs. Some alcoholics have been able to stop for quite long periods simply through an effort of will, but all too often they return to uncontrolled drinking unless they get proper help. Recovery from alcoholism is a long and often complex process which very few individuals seem able to accomplish alone and unaided.

**Q. Couldn't the alcoholic change his drinking by changing his environment?**

**A.** No, although it might bring temporary improvement. But for real recovery most alcoholics need expert help.

**Q. What about divorce? Many men who drink too much blame it on their wives.**

**A.** Since they themselves don't understand the nature of their illness, alcoholics tend to blame their uncontrolled drinking on a variety of outside things, usually beginning with their wives—or husbands. Or their jobs, or their boss. But the trouble lies within them, and changing these outside factors does not bring their drinking back under control once control has been lost.

**Q. What kind of "help" does an alcoholic need?**

**A.** First he may need medical care to get the alcohol out of his system and to make him feel well again. Practicing alcoholics never feel well; most of the time, except when anesthetized by alcohol, they feel very sick indeed, and it's pretty hard to think straight or to do anything constructive when you feel that sick. Next he needs to learn the nature of his illness, and to understand and accept it. Finally he needs understanding support while he is learning to live without alcohol in a world where it is all around him. All this adds up to treatment, for alcoholism requires treatment just like any other illness.

**Q. Is alcoholism the same in everyone?**

**A.** Most Americans have the same type of alcoholism, Gamma. Dr. Jellinek (see Chapter 1, "Facts and Figures"), in his book *The Disease Concept of Alcoholism,* classifies "the alcoholisms" under five headings: Alpha, Beta, Delta, Gamma, and Epsilon. The most prevalent type in the United States and in other English-speaking countries is Gamma, which he describes as (1) acquired increased tissue tolerance to alcohol, (2) adaptive cell metabolism, (3) withdrawal symptoms and "craving," *i.e.*, physical dependence, and (4) loss of control.

**Q. Will you describe the other types?**

**A.** *Alpha alcoholism* is a **purely** psychological **continual** dependence or reliance upon the effect of alcohol to relieve bodily or emotional pain. The drinking is undisciplined in the sense that it goes beyond the rules set by society—but it does not lead to loss of control. *Beta alcoholism* is that type in which such alcoholic complications as polyneuropathy, gastritis, and cirrhosis of the liver may occur without either physical or psychological dependence on alcohol. Alpha and Beta alcoholism may both develop into Gamma or Delta alcoholism. *Delta alcoholism* shows the first three characteristics of Gamma but, instead of loss of control, there is inability to abstain. In contrast to Gamma, there is no ability to stop drinking for even a day or two without the manifestation of withdrawal symptoms, but the ability to control the amount of intake on any given occasion remains intact. Delta alcoholism is the predominant type in France and some other countries with a large wine consumption. *Epsilon alcoholism* is periodic uncontrolled drinking.

**Q. What did Dr. Jellinek say about alcoholism being a disease?**

**A.** He said, "The current majority opinion to which the present writer subscribes, and subscribed before it was a majority opinion, is that anomalous forms of the ingestion of narcotics and alcohol, such as drinking with loss of control and physical dependence, are caused by physiopathological processes and constitute diseases."

**Q. Do certain kinds of people have certain types of alcoholism?**

**A.** No, not if we are speaking of individuals. Any kind of individual may have any type of alcoholism. As noted above, however, certain varieties of alcoholism are more common in certain countries. And there are infinite individual variations within any variety.

**Q. Is alcoholism contagious?**

**A.** Not in the usual sense that one can catch the flu from someone who has the virus, but in the broadest sense of the word there are many questions, since so many husbands and wives have developed alcoholism after living with it for years.

**Q. Is there such a thing as instant alcoholism?**

**A.** Yes, there is, although it is rare. But there are cases where full-blown alcoholism appeared at the very beginning of drinking.

**Q. Can alcoholism suddenly develop after many years of normal drinking?**

**A.** Yes, it can. Usually this can be traced to some kind of shock—a physical shock from a severe illness or an accident, or a psychological shock such as the loss of a wife or child. There are many instances of someone in his forties or fifties or older, who drank without any trouble until then, suddenly going out of control and showing all the signs of middle or even late alcoholism.

**Q. Does the quantity you drink have to do with alcoholism?**

**A.** Certainly no one will develop alcoholism if he always limits himself to small amounts. Most alcoholics seem to have started out as excessive drinkers "able to drink more than anybody else," although occasionally someone appears who from the beginning had a small capacity, never drank great quantities, and yet whose drinking went out of control. In the case of alcoholics, they lose the high tolerance with which they started, and as the disease progresses, get drunk on less and less alcohol. Nevertheless, the person who consistently drinks very large quantities is asking for trouble, and the quantity itself may well trigger alcoholism.

**Q. Does what you drink matter?**

**A.** If you mean brands, or whether it is whiskey, brandy, gin, vodka, or any other hard liquor, no it doesn't. But if you mean wine or beer as opposed to the hard stuff, then it does, since in the United States wine or beer drinkers do not seem to develop alcoholism nearly as frequently as hard-liquor drinkers.

**Q. Are convulsions ever related to alcoholism?**

**A.** Convulsions are one of the serious complications of alcoholism and are liable to come at the end of a long period of drinking—a spree or a bender. They can sometimes cause death if medical treatment is not quickly provided.

**Q. Is alcoholism a painful illness?**

**A.** In my opinion the most painful of all. Alcoholism hurts in every department of your life. Physically, the alcoholic always feels sick—very sick—except of course when he's had enough drinks not to feel anything. Mentally, the suffering is acute, because you can't stay high or drunk all the time, and at sober moments—especially about three o'clock in the morning—you know exactly what's happening to you, you see your life going down the drain, and you don't know why or what to do about it. Emotionally, it hurts terribly, since you are losing all you value and love, you are hurting those who love you, and you seem powerless to do anything about it. Socially, your life is a shambles, your friends begin to disappear, no one wants to come to see you, and they no longer invite you out. So far as your career is concerned, it's appalling, because your ability to function is gradually dwindling: whatever you do, you can no longer do it well. And financially it's a disaster. It costs so much money to drink the amount an alcoholic must have to function at all. Ask any alcoholic whether his alcoholism was painful, and I think he will agree with me.

**Q. Can alcoholism be prevented?**

**A.** The one sure way to prevent it is never to drink at all. Otherwise, since the causes are not known, there is no way to prevent it from happening to that small percentage of those who drink who are susceptible to it. We have no way of knowing which ones they are. In our present state of knowledge, the closest we can come to prevention is to try to teach everyone the earliest symptoms and hope that they will seek help before too much damage has been done.

**Q. Can an individual keep his drinking from developing into alcoholism?**

**A.** It may be possible if he catches it early enough and is willing and able to apply strict rules to his drinking. It would be much safer and surer for such a person to stop drinking altogether, and if he has not progressed beyond the earliest symptoms he may be able to do this alone. If not, then he can always seek help. And if this happens early enough, he may not have to suffer all the pain described earlier.

**Q. Are some people predisposed to alcoholism?**

**A.** No one knows for sure. But if someone had alcoholism in his family, a father or mother or uncle or aunt or grandparents, or several of these, as has been the case with many alcoholics I know, he would certainly be well-advised to take every precaution. He should learn everything he can and apply it to himself at the first signs he notices. It seems—to me at least—that no intelligent person would walk into alcoholism with his eyes open!

# 5. Recognition

**Q. Is alcoholism easily recognizable?**

**A.** It's easy enough in the late stages, which everyone recognizes. It's easy in the middle stages for those close to the alcoholic, providing they are informed enough to know what they're seeing. In other words it can be recognized, but too often isn't, partly because so many people think that only the late stages are alcoholism or that alcoholism doesn't happen to people *they* know. What is important is to recognize it in the early stages, and this is not so easy, because on the surface it looks much like other people's heavy drinking. The real problem is that alcoholism is masked by an accepted social custom—drinking, and in much of our society, heavy drinking. Nevertheless, the alcoholic inevitably begins to stand out from his fellows: his drinking is different from theirs in many subtle, small, but recognizable ways. His drinking is also increasingly different from what it used to be. The detailed symptoms (Chapter 6) will pinpoint this.

**Q. How can you recognize alcoholism?**

**A.** Even before there are noticeable behavior symptoms there are things to watch for. You must be alert to the *way* a person drinks—the drinking pattern—and notice whether there is any change in it. Alcoholism brings about continuing changes in the drinking pattern, but these are often slow and gradual and may disappear from time to time for short periods. Generally they are so gradual that most people don't notice them, even in their own husband or wife. Of course most people don't particularly want to notice the way someone else drinks unless it is way out of line, so they may be genuinely unaware that someone's drinking is changing, or his reaction to drinks is different. Should the subject come up, it's easier to find "reasons" for each evident change, such as "He's having trouble at home" or "That job is enough to make anybody take to drink" or "That boss of his is difficult" or "He's had a lousy day—or week."

When a person is consistently the last one at the bar, or begins to get drunk pretty regularly while the others in his group only get high, or when he often gets drunk at the wrong time or place, then alcoholism has undoubtedly set in.

**Q. What is a drinking pattern?**

**A.** It is a person's usual way of drinking, including amounts, times, and places. A moderate drinking pattern in some milieus, for instance, could mean very regular consumption of one or two drinks before dinner. Even where this occurs daily, such a drinker may rarely get high and never get drunk. A moderate drinking pattern may even include one drink at lunch, rarely more. A heavy drinking pattern would up the amounts and increase the times, both in duration and to include occasional part afternoons at the bar or over cards. It would also add to the places, the bar car on the commuter train, a neighborhood pub on the way home or after dinner or both, and all kinds of bars during the evening.

**Q. Families recognize it easily, don't they?**

**A.** Unfortunately, no. Too few of them know enough to know what they're seeing. Too many of them think that alcoholism can't happen to *their* family. And all of them are prevented from admitting it even to themselves by the stigma that still lies so heavily on alcoholism. A study done by NCA some years ago on wives of alcoholics revealed that the average time before they sought advice or help was eleven years after they began noticing that something was terribly wrong. First they didn't know *what* was wrong, second they were afraid to talk about it to anyone, and third they didn't know where to go for help. Some eventually went to clergymen, some to lawyers, a very few to doctors.

**Q. Is it possible to recognize the earliest symptoms?**

**A.** In yourself, yes. You have only to know what they are and to be honest with yourself. And it is certainly to your advantage to be honest! But it is difficult to recognize them in someone else, because so many of them have to do with *feelings* about drinking: a need for drinks at certain times, a need for drinks in order to enjoy other things, in short a *need* for drinks—dependence. Certain behavior symptoms can be recognized also—gulping drinks, consistently drinking more than other people, change in personality and in reactions to people and the current situation, whatever it is, and a gradually changing drinking pattern. More detailed symptoms will be found in the next chapter.

**Q. How can an employer recognize alcoholism in an employee?**

**A.** By his deteriorating work performance and his deteriorating relations with others on the job. These in fact are the only ways an employer should try to recognize alcoholism, for he has no right to act as a diagnostician of an illness. But he does have a right to expect satisfactory job performance, productivity, and good work relations from his employees. When an employee has alcoholism these are the areas where it will show up on the job, and it is on this basis that the problem should be handled. It can be well handled this way too, especially where the company has good disciplinary procedures. In a small business, or one which has a less formal organizational structure, it can often be handled on a personal basis, with the employee sent to an outside doctor "to find out what's wrong that's affecting your work," or to a member of Alcoholics Anonymous who may work there or be a friend of the employer or of the employee. The employer may not be too sure that his recognition of these signs is really alcoholism, and he needs expert advice. It just could be something else, although the chances are that it is not.

**Q. Can a fellow worker recognize alcoholism?**

**A.** Probably more surely than the boss, for he may well see the employee outside, may often drink with him and therefore have had a chance to observe his drinking pattern and his reactions to drinking, in addition to having noticed his changing personality and work performance.

**Q. Can a friend recognize it?**

**A.** Even more surely than the fellow worker, unless the latter is also a good friend. His contacts with the alcoholic will probably include many drinking occasions when he has the opportunity to observe all the changes detailed above.

**Q. Why are families so reluctant to recognize alcoholism?**

**A.** Often they simply can't believe it on the basis of their limited knowledge. And they quite naturally don't want to believe it. The stigma is an immense factor, for alcoholism is too widely considered a family disgrace. The "hopeless drunk" myth also makes them prefer to hide it since they don't think anything can be done about it anyway. But I think that the shame which the alcoholic's behavior so often makes them feel, helps to drive them underground, where they join the conspiracy of silence about the whole thing, just hoping that no one will know.

**Q. Why are companies so reluctant to recognize this particular illness?**

**A.** Companies, which are made up of people, are affected by all the myths and misconceptions common to the rest of us, and are equally ignorant of even the simplest facts about alcoholism. Many of them find it hard to believe they have any alcoholics in their employ, carrying the image of the Skid Row bum or at least of the last stages of alcoholism, when the alcoholic would be patently unemployable. They have been largely unaware that they have been paying a heavy premium for concealment, for everyone in the company has been "protecting" his particular alcoholic, giving him "just one more chance," talking to him like a Dutch uncle, covering up for him, and all because "He's such a good guy," "He has a wonderful family," or, even more often, "He's the best worker in the department, or office, or business—when he's sober." Meanwhile the progression has inevitably gone on, sometimes for years and years, work performance has steadily declined, productivity has dwindled, no one wants to be around him anymore, and finally he reaches the last stages, is definitely unemployable, and is fired. Meanwhile the company has been paying him at the level he reached before the alcoholism began to take its toll, and although he might have been passed over for promotions, he probably, if he was a union man, got all the raises the others did. And the unions behaved the same way about him that management did; after all, they are made up of people too, uninformed people just like the management people. Fortunately, all this is changing, and one day soon employed alcoholics will have a better chance of recovery than housewives, professionals, artists, writers, etc.

**Q. Why is society so reluctant to recognize alcoholism?**

**A.** For all the reasons that all the above-named are reluctant, and more besides. Society is all of the people, and where the majority view is strongly held, as our old views of alcoholism and alcoholics were, the rest tend to go along with it. So we have condemned the alcoholic, and in reality, too often, we have sentenced him to death. One of society's overriding reasons, in my opinion, for being so reluctant to recognize alcoholism for what it is, and the alcoholic for what he is, a desperately sick individual who is the unwitting and unwilling victim of something he did not seek and does not want, is that looking hard at the alcoholic's drinking might make them have to look at their own. And people are very sensitive and protective about their own drinking.

**Q. What can be done to make the recognition of alcoholism more widespread?**

**A.** More public information, more education both in general and in depth. The National Council on Alcoholism launched such a program in 1944, and it continues, and must continue until public attitudes change and everyone has at least the basic information about alcoholism necessary to remove the unwarranted stigma and to make it possible for an alcoholic and/or his family to seek help without shame, and to know where to go to get that help. And then of course the help must be there, which means an informed and willing medical profession, adequate treatment facilities, better understanding of A.A. and how to use its immensely valuable services, and a host of other things that will follow when attitudes really change.

# 6. Symptoms

**Q. What are the symptoms of alcoholism?**

**A.** There is a different set of symptoms at each of the different stages in the progression of the disease, but the one common symptom when alcoholism has really set in is loss of control over drinking.

**Q. What is meant by "loss of control"?**

**A.** When a person drinks more than he intended to, *i.e.*, gets drunk when others do not; or gets drunk at the wrong time or place, or gets drunk when his avowed intention was to have just one or two, or drinks to drunkenness when he had promised himself he wasn't going to drink that day, or evening, or on that occasion.

**Q. What are the different stages of alcoholism?**

**A.** For convenience they can be divided into early, middle, and late. The lines between each stage are not sharp and clear; rather they tend to overlap so that it is often not noticeable for a while that someone has progressed to another stage.

**Q. What are the early symptoms?**

**A.** These are the symptoms which are largely invisible to others because most of them manifest themselves as feelings rather than behavior. The major and initial one is the reaction of the individual to alcohol when he first discovers it: *it's magic*. It performs miracles for him. It magics away his discomforts, his anxieties, his fears. It gives him instant self-confidence. And so it immediately becomes terribly important to him. He *needs* it. It makes him feel like the kind of person he wants to be. There are many other symptoms, a number of which involve behavior, but they can all be lumped together as an increasing dependence on alcohol to help him do what others are doing, or learning to do, without a chemical aid, *i.e.*, solve the problems of growing up, whether they are of shyness or boredom or apprehension or frustration or lack of confidence or any other problem of living.

**Q. But you say there are many behavior symptoms. Can't these be seen?**

**A.** Yes, but they are not easily recognized unless you are alerted to them. Gulping drinks and the ability to outdrink others are visible but usually misinterpreted. So is a growing insistence on having a large amount of time allotted to drinking before dinner; or on not going to places which don't serve liquor, public or private; or lying about the amount consumed, always minimizing it; or going to great lengths to make sure drinks are available for any special event—a football game or a picnic on the beach, etc. The alcoholic also tends to insist that he *must* drink to calm his nerves or because he's had such a hard day or because he's depressed or even because something unusually good has happened—a raise or a promotion, for example. His behavior while drinking and about drinking is really different, but not yet in such obvious or bizarre ways that anyone notices it—unless they're looking for it and know what it means. Then, too, one or two of these things alone are not enough to be sure it's early alcoholism; there must be a cluster of them, including behavioral, psychological, and physical.

**Q. What are some of the psychological symptoms?**

**A.** Many of the behavior symptoms are also psychological, meaning the drinker's feeling of need for alcohol and his growing dependence on it. There are certain psychological signs of a dawning compulsion to drink—when the drinker may well recognize that drinking is not appropriate at that time or place but drinks nevertheless, or when he agrees verbally that one or two should be enough yet seems driven to make it three, four, or five.

**Q. You mentioned physical symptoms. What are these?**

**A.** They are few in the early stage but would seem to indicate a difference in the way the alcoholic's body handles alcohol. For instance, he rarely has a hangover; he rarely gets actively sick while drinking; he rarely shows the usual physical effects (thickening of speech, "rubber legs," passing out) of the unusually large amount of liquor he is able to consume. He sometimes has blackouts even this early.

**Q. What is a blackout?**

**A.** A blackout is not to be confused with passing out, which is unconsciousness. In a blackout the person walks and talks, apparently normally, but has no recollection of it afterward. It is a form of amnesia and is one of the most terrifying things that happen to alcoholics.

**Q. Shouldn't everyone be taught these earliest symptoms before he begins drinking?**

**A.** I certainly think so, because we have no way of knowing which of those who will drink will be the ones to get alcoholism. I think it's not fair to children, who supposedly are being prepared to meet life and its problems, to leave them totally unprepared for this one. They're bound to meet it, if not in themselves then in someone close to them, perhaps the person they marry, or even their own children. I think we have a responsibility to teach all children these crucial facts.

**Q. How long do these last before the middle stage is reached?**

**A.** An average of ten years. But this is an average, and as with all generalizations it must be recognized that there are exceptions. It could be five or six, and it could be twelve or fifteen. And all during that time there is a steady progression, so that it isn't a big leap from one stage to the next, with dramatic changes evident overnight. It's rather a series of small changes, a gradual accumulation.

**Q. Do the middle symptoms become visible?**

**A.** In large part, yes. For instance the behavior symptoms have markedly increased both in number and in noticeability. Among the new behavior symptoms are an increased consumption—an increased number of drinking times per day. Signs of having been drinking now show often, and at the wrong times. Weekends frequently turn into drinking bouts, or benders. There are increasing signs of irritability when not drinking. Blackouts occur more frequently and closer together. Hangovers also increase and become acute; they are so extreme for the alcoholic that they really should have a different name: no normal drinker would recognize them as what he has. By now the alcoholic cannot function without a steady supply of alcohol and begins to protect his supply. His preoccupation with drinking is so great that it interferes with everything, it is never out of his mind. And he has lost control. The fact that something is terribly wrong is now evident to almost everyone who knows him at all well.

**Q. How long does the middle stage last?**

**A.** Anywhere from two to five years is average. But there are many cases where it has lasted ten to fifteen years, due to outside circumstances—perhaps professional discipline or a home life that has been tailored to helping him conceal his problem and deal with it or a job which permits him to conceal the amount he drinks yet provides some outside discipline.

**Q. What are the late symptoms?**

**A.** They can be summed up easily: he lives to drink and drinks to live. He is now drinking because of his drinking. He cannot function without it in any way, and often he drinks to the exclusion of eating. He is nearly always drunk, even though he doesn't always appear so. He often does what he calls "drinking himself sober." He is a slob, and he no longer cares. He is the world's picture of the alcoholic.

**Q. Can alcoholism be arrested at any point along this spectrum?**

**A.** Yes, it can. But at this point in time it is easiest to do this in the middle stages, since the alcoholic is still reachable by many people in his world, and he must be reached and brought to want help. This is an illness in which his full and conscious cooperation is essential. There is no way to stick him with a needle and bring about his recovery, and there is no magic pill. But he can recover, with help, if he will accept that help. And this has happened in the early and in the late stages as well.

**Q. It should be easier to treat in the early stages, shouldn't it?**

**A.** Yes, and it is, providing such a person can be motivated to want help. And more and more of them are as the kind of information in this book is becoming more widely known. In the early days of Alcoholics Anonymous, in the late thirties, the members were well over forty, and anyone under forty was not considered to be a good bet. Now the majority of people coming to A.A. are in their early forties or in their thirties. And there are an increasing number in their twenties, some in their teens. This is a measure of what education is doing.

**Q. At what stage do most alcoholics seek help?**

**A.** The middle stage, and more and more in the early part of the middle stage, before they have begun to lose jobs, families, and self-respect.

**Q. Can alcoholism be successfully treated even in the late stage?**

**A.** Apparently it can, although most people believed until recently that those on Skid Row or those who came regularly before the courts were too far gone. With recent carefully planned efforts such as those in Atlanta, Georgia; Denver, Colorado; New York City, and the District of Columbia, we are beginning to see hopeful results with last-stage alcoholics. There is no question however that the chances are much less good with people who have deteriorated to this extent, and the time involved and, accordingly, the costs are much greater. If we, the people, are willing to pay for it, I believe that there is much that can be done for this group of alcoholics. And we, the taxpayers, will benefit, for in this group of nonproductive indigents there are some who can become employed, taxpaying, responsible citizens, thus lessening by a considerable amount the tax burden they now impose. Further, we as a humane people will benefit, for we will be giving this group of very sick people a chance at recovery and a decent life.

# 7. The Alcoholic

**Q. What is "the alcoholic"?**

**A.** Anyone whose drinking causes a *continuing* problem in any department of his or her life. The word "continuing" is the key word. Many people may have problems because of their drinking at one time or another in their lives. In order to get rid of the problems they will do something about the drinking—either cutting it down or cutting it out. They *can* do this, and they do. That's what the alcoholic tries to do—but he can't. He has lost control.

**Q. How did they come to be called alcoholics?**

**A.** The word *alcoholic* and its companion word *alcoholism* were coined in 1848 by a Swedish scientist named Dr. Magnus Huss. Prior to that time the condition was referred to as chronic or continual drunkenness, and the victim of the condition as a drunkard. These terms were more descriptive than scientific, and Dr. Huss apparently felt the need for scientific terminology; at any rate he coined the terms and they gradually came to replace all others. In the United States they were slower to gain acceptance than in Europe, and for many years, until well after the turn of the century, the favored terms were *inebriate* and *inebriety*. *Dipsomania* and *dipsomaniac* were also widely used then. Today *alcoholism* and *alcoholic* are the near-universal choice, although industry and some therapists prefer another descriptive term—*problem drinker*.

**Q. Is the alcoholic a particular type of person?**

**A.** No. Alcoholics are all kinds of people: from rich to poor, from highly intelligent to ignorant, and from every walk of life. Since alcoholism is a disease, it is no respecter of persons and knows no boundaries, geographic, economic, social, or of sex, race, color, or creed. Alcoholism strikes human beings whoever or wherever they are—workers, executives, professionals, clergymen, housewives, career women, the famous, and the great anonymous masses. No one who drinks is immune.

**Q. Is there any ethnic background that makes one more or less immune?**

**A.** Studies indicate that alcoholism is less prevalent among Jewish people and most prevalent among Irish-Americans. The reasons for this are not known although there are many theories.

**Q. Is there an alcoholic personality?**

**A.** No. Considerable research has failed to produce any evidence that there is such a thing. The belief in such a possibility undoubtedly stems from many striking similarities in full-blown alcoholics—in behavior, in speech, in thinking and feeling. But many therapists believe that the neurotic pattern of the alcoholic is the result of alcoholism, rather than inherent in the person. This belief is supported by the fact that so many alcoholics return to normal effective functioning when they stop drinking, with a minimum of psychiatric treatment, or none at all.

**Q. Why do so many still think *the* alcoholic is the Skid Row bum?**

**A.** Probably because this is the most visible part of the alcoholic population, even though it is only a small percentage of the total. Since most of these men are in the late stages of alcoholism, there is no doubt as to their condition. Furthermore, it is out in the open and can be seen by all, whereas the wealthy man in the late stages is protected by his environment. Even those who may be in a very low financial bracket usually have families who care for them.

**Q. Is there a way to tell whether you are an alcoholic?**

**A.** Yes, there is a simple test. It is generally impossible for an alcoholic to control his drinking over any long period of time, although he can "go on the wagon" temporarily, sometimes for quite lengthy periods. The secret is control—the alcoholic has lost it. The test is: for a period of six months, *at least,* determine not to exceed a certain number of drinks a day, that number to be not more than three. (This does not mean it *has* to be daily.) Whatever number is chosen, one, two, or three, must not be exceeded under any circumstances. Absolutely no exceptions, or the test is failed. This test has shown many people they had alcoholism, and has relieved the minds of many more who had no difficulty in passing it.

**Q. Are most alcoholics loners?**

**A.** No. Most alcoholics are gregarious and prefer drinking with others. However, they may do a lot of quick drinking by themselves before they join the others. And when on a real bender an alcoholic may hole up at home or in a hotel room to drink. In the late stages most alcoholics drink alone, but it is as much because other people avoid them as vice versa.

**Q. Can you tell an alcoholic by looking?**

**A.** Not usually, until he's in the late stages. There are a few signs which begin to appear in the late middle stage, but most people don't notice them—a certain puffiness, and a coarseness of the skin on the hands; a nonclear white of the eye, sometimes a tiny bit reddish; and occasionally enlarged pores in the nose. Of course these signs may have other causes and taken singly do not constitute a "diagnosis" of alcoholism, but where all of them are present either at once or separately, there is certainly cause for suspicion of alcoholism.

**Q. Can a teenager be an alcoholic?**

**A.** It can happen, but it's not usual. The average time it takes for alcoholism to show itself is ten years of drinking, and few children begin before ten! Of course there are the rare instant alcoholics, who are full-blown from their first drink, which may be as early as fourteen or fifteen. It is my opinion, however, that in all cases the alcoholism may well be there from the first drink or even before it, and that recognition of the earliest, invisible symptoms could stop the course of the illness before any damage was done. That is why I believe we must have better teaching in the schools and at home, and why everyone should know those earliest symptoms before he begins to drink.

**Q. Do most alcoholics have families?**

**A.** Most men do, and their families stand by them a very long time. Friends, too, stick with the alcoholic for a long time. Alcoholics, by and large, are very nice people.

**Q. Why is the alcoholic so determined to solve his problem by himself?**

**A.** It's partly our national heritage of independence —we are expected to take care of our own problems. But alcoholism wouldn't fall into this category if it were recognized as a disease. It is largely because we think of it as a weakness—a matter of will—that we expect people to handle it by themselves. And the alcoholic shares that common view—and tries . . . and tries . . . and tries . . . and fails, because it *is* a disease and he needs expert help.

# 8.

# The Woman Alcoholic

**Q. Are there many women alcoholics?**

**A.** Approximately one fifth as many as men. This ratio is borne out by admission figures from public clinics and state hospitals, but many doctors in private practice report that they see as many women as men, so the ratio may be higher than thought.

**Q. Why would there be such a difference?**

**A.** The proportion of women who drink is lower than the proportion of men, so fewer women are exposed to alcoholism. But even more important is the fact that the stigma on alcoholism, which is still very great, is about twice as heavy for women as for men. We have a double standard for women: in general they are expected to behave better than men, and in some areas behavior that is permissible for men is absolutely unacceptable for women. Drinking is an outstanding example of this double standard. A man's having too much to drink in public is often laughed at or shrugged off, but for a woman it is unthinkable behavior. This means that when a woman feels uncertain about her drinking—when her control is beginning to slip—she goes underground. She will drink very little in public and then finish a bottle when she gets home. She will do most of her drinking at home, and if she is a housewife she can nip all day unobserved. And if and when she seeks help she will go to a doctor or clergyman, since this can be kept confidential.

**Q. Are women alcoholics different from men alcoholics?**

**A.** They often appear to be quite different, but this is more apparent than real. There is no difference in the way the disease affects them—it is the same disease. The many apparent differences are usually due to the different circumstances in which most women do their drinking.

**Q. Are the early symptoms the same in women?**

**A.** Yes. And just as in men, they are largely invisible. But they are easily recognizable if the woman knows what to look for and is able to be honest with herself.

**Q. Are any of the behavior symptoms different?**

**A.** Yes, again because of her different circumstances and the fact of her being a woman. This is particularly true if she is a housewife. If she is a career woman, her behavior symptoms will be much closer to those of a man, because her way of living is similar to that of a man's. But there are enough similarities even in a protected housewife so that recognition is equally possible, especially for those close to her—her own family, for instance.

**Q. Is it more difficult to reach women alcoholics?**

**A.** Definitely yes. They are first of all more protected, and so the condition may not be known beyond their own front door. Most husbands will go to even greater lengths than wives to conceal this. And finally, the woman is all too aware of the stigma and feels a sense of shame and disgrace that drives her into deep hiding. She usually has the greatest resistance to accepting outside help, and will avoid it or refuse it sometimes unto death. And even when in treatment she is apt to be more difficult than a man. Her whole pattern of concealment, evasion, and lying is so deeply ingrained that it is hard for her to overcome it. And alcoholics cannot be helped until they are able to openly come to grips with their situation, and to accept their condition. Fortunately, more and more women are doing this, and recovering, and this in turn gives those still suffering, courage and hope.

**Q. Is it just as easy for women to recover?**

**A.** Yes, today it is, and this is largely due to the increasing general acceptance of alcoholism as a disease rather than a disgrace, and to the increasing number of women who have recovered.

**Q. Do many women join Alcoholics Anonymous?**

**A.** Yes. A.A. has estimated that about one fourth of its membership of 425,000 are women—more than 106,000.

**Q. Are most women alcoholics career women?**

**A.** No, most are housewives, just as most of our female population are. But there are many career women, professional women, actresses, writers, etc., in A.A.

**Q. Are most women alcoholics wealthy?**

**A.** No, they follow the pattern of our general population and come from every economic level.

**Q. Do most women alcoholics still have their families?**

**A.** No. Of course some do, but although most have been married they have too often been divorced by the time they seek help. Men generally will not put up with an alcoholic wife as women will with an alcoholic husband. And all too frequently these women have lost their children. Of course no one knows how many women whose alcoholism is still active are also still married. These are the ones whose husbands and families are still succeeding in concealment. But if the known pattern holds they will be divorced or deserted as their illness progresses.

**Q. At what age do most women alcoholics seek help?**

**A.** The late thirties and early forties. Many come later of course, and in recent years there has been a heartening increase in the number of women in their twenties who seek help. Today the age level is about the same with women as with men.

# 9. Causes

**Q. What causes alcoholism?**

**A.** No one really knows, although there are many theories. Experts in the field are generally agreed, however, that there is no single cause such as a germ or a virus or alcohol itself. If alcohol alone were the cause, everyone who drank would develop alcoholism, and this is obviously not true. It seems to depend on the man, not the bottle, plus a consistently large intake. The consensus is that the causes will be found in all of three areas—physiological, psychological, and social.

**Q. Isn't it sometimes called an allergy?**

**A.** Yes it is, but not by scientists. This is a word that has been used largely by Alcoholics Anonymous, but most of those who use it are aware that it is being used in a very large sense as it often is in the language. There was a movie, for instance, called *Allergic to Love,* and people commonly say, "Joan is allergic to John" or "He is allergic to parties." Medically speaking, alcoholics are not allergic to alcohol, or they probably wouldn't drink it.

**Q. Could there be a difference in the bodily chemistry of the alcoholic?**

**A.** It is possible, and there is a great deal of research being done in an effort to find such a difference. Modern techniques have unearthed many clues indicating that what has been called the "X factor" may one day be found, but to date there is no proof that such a physical cause exists. Should it be discovered it would make it far easier to bring alcoholism under control, for there could then be no question as to its being a disease and the stigma still impeding progress would inevitably fade away, allowing alcoholics to admit their illness freely since it no longer would mark them as "weaklings" or as victims of a self-inflicted condition.

**Q. Don't some people think it's just a neurosis?**

**A.** Yes, and in particular many psychiatrists think this. But most psychiatrists active in the field or who have treated many alcoholics believe that the undoubted psychological components of alcoholism may well be the results of the illness rather than the cause of it. Here again there is no proof. No scientific research has succeeded in pinpointing any specific psychological causes that are common to all alcoholics, and the search for "the alcoholic personality" has been unsuccessful. Until there are good longitudinal studies taking 2,000 or 3,000 twelve-year-olds and following them well into their forties, this will remain an open question.

**Q. What is meant by social causes?**

**A.** Cultural attitudes toward drinking as well as cultural drinking habits, plus general and specific environments—the world in which the individual is born, grows up, and lives, and to which, by and large, he tends to conform. It is thought that cultural attitudes toward drinking may have a great bearing on the incidence of alcoholism. Studies indicate that it is very low among Jews, for instance, who have a very clear and unambiguous attitude toward alcohol: it is good, and wine has an important place in many of their religious observances; but they have equally clear social sanctions against the abuse or misuse of this good thing. This is in great contrast to attitudes growing out of the Puritan ethic, where uncertainty and guilt surround the use of alcohol, yet there is great permissiveness toward its overuse. The incidence of alcoholism is correspondingly high.

**Q. How can permissiveness toward heavy drinking and drunkenness help to create alcoholism?**

**A.** No one knows to just what extent heavy drinking and frequent drunkenness contribute to the development of alcoholism, but it's certain that you don't get alcoholism without these. I've never heard of a moderate drinker who became an alcoholic, unless that moderate drinking grew into heavy drinking which then continued for a long time with more than occasional drunkenness. Alcohol in large amounts is a toxic substance, and the body must readjust to handle it. This can bring about tissue changes which make the body need more of the substance to which it has now adjusted. Many scientists believe this to be an important factor in the development of alcoholism. Where there is permissiveness toward this kind of drinking, therefore, more people are going to be exposed to the danger of alcoholism.

**Q. Are there specific environmental causes?**

**A.** It is thought that growing up in a family where one or both parents are practicing alcoholics may lead to alcoholism on the part of the children. There are other environmental situations which may also be conducive to the development of alcoholism, such as being part of an adolescent group which drinks heavily or choosing an occupation where heavy drinking is the norm. Children from broken homes are also thought to be more prone to alcoholism. It is certain that lack of attention by parents, and the failure to set limits for adolescents who are trying to learn to live in this world, lay them open to many hazards, of which alcoholism is a major one.

**Q. Can alcoholism appear even where environmental causes are not present?**

**A.** Yes, it can. There are alcoholics who came from well-adjusted, happy families, who had an apparently normal satisfying childhood and adolescence, who made good starts at good careers, and yet were struck down by alcoholism. These are some of the many baffling, mysterious things about this illness. One day it is to be hoped that research will give us some of these answers.

**Q. Isn't it just a matter of bad behavior?**

**A.** No, it is much more complicated than that. Alcoholics don't really want to behave badly, and suffer intense remorse over their own behavior. Most of them express extreme loathing toward themselves, and castigate themselves for being "bad." Their dearest wish is to drink "like other people" and not to get into trouble because of their drinking.

**Q. Wouldn't a strong will prevent alcoholism from developing?**

**A.** Apparently not, since most alcoholics have a very strong will regarding areas other than drinking. In the case of drinking they have what amounts to a compulsion, and this is a very powerful drive, so strong and so deep-seated that it overpowers even the strongest will.

# 10.

# Denial or the Alibi System

**Q. Is there any particularly outstanding characteristic of alcoholics?**

**A.** Yes. Denial. Almost without exception alcoholics deny their condition and continue to do so long after it has become apparent to everyone around them. Everyone knows the alcoholic's insistence that "I can take it or leave it alone." But he almost never leaves it alone.

**Q. Why do they do this?**

**A.** There are many reasons. Perhaps the most important, and most overlooked, is the universal human reluctance to being "different." Everyone wants to be able to do the things other people can do, especially when they are pleasant things, and drinking is generally considered to be one of man's great pleasures. It's hard for anyone to have to give this up even though it has long ceased being a pleasure and has become extremely painful. It must be remembered that drinking was unusually pleasurable (magic) for the alcoholic in his early drinking days and this memory haunts him. His entire effort is to recapture those early feelings, and his dogged persistence in this effort is enhanced by the fact that he occasionally manages to do so, even in the last stage of alcoholism. Every now and then the pain and the sickness is interrupted by a "good" drinking day, and his hopes soar high that maybe *now* he can drink again "the way he used to." So he will go on, even though the next month or months are unadulterated pain and trouble. The time never comes when these magic moments do not unexpectedly recur, albeit at greater and greater intervals and for shorter and shorter times.

**Q. What are some of the other reasons?**

**A.** Sheer ignorance about alcoholism is one. If they haven't lost everything they can't be an alcoholic. If they're not on Skid Row they can't be an alcoholic. If they still have a job and money they can't be an alcoholic. And they really believe these things, which is no wonder considering it's exactly what their world —and their families—believe. Alcoholics are very good citizens: they conform absolutely to prevailing public opinion about their own condition. Then too, most alcoholics are unaware that it is impossible for them to control their drinking once that control is lost. In their ignorance, most alcoholics spend their energies in trying, devising elaborate means for achieving their goal: switching drinks—from whiskey to gin, from spirits to sherry or wine or beer; never drinking at home, or never drinking away from home; never drinking after dinner or never drinking before dinner; drinking milk before they drink alcohol; taking immense amounts of vitamins; eating lots of steaks—and a host of other devices. None of them work, since the loss of control effectively prevents their working. And the ignorant alcoholic is completely baffled. So baffled and confused in fact that he fears for his sanity. This is a very real and terrible fear for many alcoholics. They are aware of how their drinking is changing, but they can't understand why and it frightens them. They know they still have control in all other areas of their lives—why not in drinking? They attempt to convince *themselves* that things are still all right, and invent "reasons" why their drinking went out of control each time it happens. And since the validity of these "reasons" is crucial to their own ability to continue functioning, they manage to believe them. These are often called "alibis" or "rationalizations," but they are actually designed more to allay the alcoholic's own fears than to convince anyone else. Nevertheless, they are so numerous, and often so ingenious, that they are known as "the alibi system."

**Q. Does stigma affect denial?**

**A.** Yes, and it plays a crucial role. Particularly the careless use of the opprobrious word *weakling.* To ask an alcoholic to label himself with that word is equivalent to asking him to put on a huge sandwich board with letters a foot high reading "I am a weakling" and to parade up and down the streets with it. No one would be willing to do this; and in the alcoholic's case he knows better anyway: he is *not* a weakling. Stigma has other unfortunate connotations: the shame and disgrace associated with this illness make it something to be avoided at all costs; the reluctance to talk about it openly allows the alcoholic also to avoid it; and the even greater reluctance to mention it to him aids and abets his own frantic efforts at concealment. In allowing the stigma to continue, the world conspires with the alcoholic to permit the inexorable progression of his disease to go on unhindered. It is cruelty of the first order.

**Q. Is there any way to break through this denial?**

**A.** Yes, there are many ways to try, and often they are successful. They will be dealt with under "Approaches to the Alcoholic" (Chapter 11).

**Q. Do families usually accept these denials?**

**A.** Families accept them for far too long, usually. They are very eager themselves that their husband, or wife, should not be "different," especially in this appalling way, and they too find "reasons" each time an episode occurs. They are perhaps even more baffled at the changes that are occurring before their eyes and struggle even harder than the alcoholic to explain them to themselves. And they are most of all affected by the stigma—the shame and the disgrace. They cover up for their alcoholic insofar as they are able, calling the office to describe his "gastritis," calling friends to apologize and explain his behavior, keeping him at home and explaining their absence from a much-anticipated dinner, refusing to listen to other members of the family who want to point out his shortcomings, and so on *ad infinitum.* They will often go to the very end of their ability to accept the alcoholic's denials, adding those of their own. They think they are "protecting" someone they love, when they are actually *preventing* his getting help.

**Q. Do friends accept the denials too?**

**A.** They will frequently go just as far as the family, and for the same reasons. However, they are more likely to come to the end of their ability to accept what they finally see as excuses, much sooner than the family, and to make an effort to speak plainly about the matter, even if they don't know too much about it. Sometimes friends make an effort to find out before speaking, so that they will have something constructive to suggest. When this happens they are in an excellent position to make a dent in the alcoholic: he is more likely to listen to them. This is undoubtedly why "friends" top the list of people given by alcoholics as the reason why they have come to Alcoholics Anonymous or an Alcoholism Information Center or a clinic.

**Q. Do employers and fellow workers accept the denials?**

**A.** Yes, and with greater alacrity than families or friends. Of course they don't see the alcoholic's off-the-job behavior, his evenings or mornings, so they are not as aware as those closer to him of the extent of the changes that are occurring. But they are just as anxious not to see him as "different," particularly as he is usually an extremely good worker and they don't want to lose him.

**Q. Does the whole community accept these denials?**

**A.** Yes, with very few exceptions. In fact, the community goes further: it denies the existence of the problem. It has been said that communities have the disease of alcoholism, since they also have the main presenting symptom—denial. It has also been pointed out that in this area communities are anti-therapeutic, since their denial effectively prevents the problem from being brought out into the open, where it can be constructively dealt with.

**Q. What can we do to change this unrealistic acceptance?**

**A.** Eliminate the stigma. Inform people by every means we have of reaching them. Organize our communities to an all-out attack on alcoholism so that there will be continuous educational programs aimed at changing attitudes. This is what the National Council on Alcoholism is trying to do.

**Q. What difference will it make if attitudes really change?**

**A.** Alcoholics would not be able to hide the nature of their difficulty for so long. Families would feel free to seek help, since there would be no shame in it. And there would be adequate facilities for diagnosis and treatment. Alcoholism would be regarded in the same way as other dread diseases, and all alcoholics would have a chance to recover.

# 11. Approaches to the Alcoholic

**Q. How can you make an alcoholic seek help?**

**A.** You can't make him. Only circumstances can make him, and then only if he is left alone to face the full consequences of his drinking, to pay the price of not seeking help. You can perhaps lead him, or persuade him, but this may have to be very subtle and indirect, and takes time. It also takes knowledge, determination, and ingenuity, for there is no simple method, no easy proven technique, no established way that automatically works with every alcoholic. In short, it's a big job, and you will need to prepare yourself if you want to tackle it. There is one universal rule for everyone who wants to help an alcoholic: *inform yourself.* Learn about alcoholism, what it is, what it does to people, how it can be treated. Learn about all the resources in your community—where they are, what they offer, what they cost. Visit them yourself, and talk to the people who counsel or treat alcoholics. Go to some A.A. meetings and listen to alcoholics talk about themselves and their feelings. Go to Al-Anon meetings (see Chapter 14, "Al-Anon and Alateen"). Then you may be ready to try to break through the alcoholic's "wall of defiance" to that suffering, terrified human being who is cowering behind it.

**Q. Is information then the most important thing?**

**A.** No, attitudes are equally important. Check your own attitudes: anyone who harbors even a tiny bit of prejudice or hostility is automatically disqualified as an effective helper. Remember that most of us have been brain-washed by the prevailing cultural attitudes, often without realizing it. Even if you have learned all there is to know about alcoholism, you will be unable to reach the alcoholic while prejudice or hostility is present, because the alcoholic will instantly detect your feeling even behind a barrage of correct, well-informed words. In this sense alcoholics are like children and dogs: they hear your feelings far more clearly than they hear your words, and it is your feelings that they respond to. It is as if their nerve ends were extended way out from their bodies, probing for affection or rejection.

**Q. Can anyone do this?**

**A.** Yes, anyone who really wants to. Such people have sometimes been mere acquaintances—neighbors perhaps, or someone working in the same office. Often it has been a nurse, sometimes a doctor or a clergyman. Most often it has been a friend.

**Q. Is a family member the best one to help?**

**A.** Not always, although they are in the best position to help because they know the whole situation better than anyone else could. Sometimes, however, the situation is so bad, and they are so filled with resentment and hostility toward the alcoholic, whom they blame for the whole thing, that they cannot hope to reach him until their attitudes have changed. This of course can and does happen as they learn the truth about his condition and the resulting behavior, and then they are in an ideal position to help. After all, they probably really love him, and in his heart he knows this, so their approach to him is not completely blocked off. Too often, however, families barge in like a bull in a china shop, having made no effort to learn what they're up against, and then they are unable to handle his denials, his protestations and promises, his defiance and his fears. When families have fully accepted the fact that their alcoholic is suffering from a deadly disease through no fault of his own, not only their attitudes but their actions change, and this in turn produces a different reaction from the alcoholic.

**Q. What else can families do?**

**A.** They can stop being protective and allow the alcoholic to face the realities of his situation. No alcoholic will stop as long as he is protected in his drinking. This does not mean punishing him; he is doing that already. But it does mean being firm. They should never threaten unless they are prepared to carry it out, and even if they do leave him, or put him out, there should always be hope involved: ". . . until you have stopped drinking" or ". . . until you have been sober six months." This mule needs a carrot too. Such drastic action should never be taken lightly, and only as a last resort, but it often provides the necessary crisis to bring an alcoholic to act on his own behalf. Families should realize too that the other helping people—doctors, clinic staffs, clergymen, A.A. members—do not have access to the alcoholic. They need an intermediary, and families can best play this role.

**Q. Can the children help?**

**A.** Often they are the key to motivating the alcoholic, and this without necessarily having any knowledge at all. One man tells of what moved him to seek help: his four-year-old daughter refused to get on his lap.

"You smell bad, Daddy," she said, "I don't like to get near you." A woman describes how her ten-year-old son planted himself before her and said, "You're always drunk and I hate you." Other ten-year-olds and many teen-agers have presented themselves at Alcoholism Information Centers asking to be told what to do, and following through carefully and well. A good many recovered alcoholics ascribe their initial realization that they must act to the words or behavior of their children. Children understand more at an earlier age than we think possible, and they are totally uninhibited in expressing themselves about it. When they're old enough to seek information, they accept the disease concept without hesitation and with conviction—it makes sense to them—and they can often convey their conviction to the alcoholic with happy results.

**Q. Can a friend help motivate the alcoholic?**

**A.** Perhaps better than anyone else, particularly if the friend has taken the trouble to inform himself. People listen to their friends, even if they give them an argument. And the friend probably doesn't have a background of bickering, nagging, pleading, and threatening, as the husband or wife usually does. He can speak his piece without the alcoholic's having much of a comeback. And what he says will make an impression, even if the alcoholic appears to reject it all and to reject him too. The friend takes the risk of losing the alcoholic's friendship, but he would lose it anyway if the disease continued unchecked, and should the alcoholic seek and find help, his gratitude to that friend will be so great that the friendship will be stronger than ever.

**Q. How about doctors?**

**A.** They are in a perfect position to motivate the alcoholic toward recovery. In the first place they can make a medical diagnosis, which the alcoholic cannot toss off. Secondly, they can outline a program for him and give it to him as a prescription for getting well. Most important of all is their ability, as doctors, to convince him that he is genuinely sick and that he cannot hope to get well unless he follows orders.

**Q. What can ministers or priests do?**

**A.** If the alcoholic can be persuaded to see them, they can do a lot. But they must know what they're doing if they're going to be effective. They cannot preach at the alcoholic or lecture him. And it will do no good to pray over him. If they understand this illness they will know how to talk to him, to make him feel that he has a real friend who cares what happens to him and wants to help him in his troubles. Then, with this kind of rapport established, they can emphasize the seriousness of this illness and the need for expert help, making concrete suggestions about a doctor, a clinic, or meeting a member of A.A. whom they may know. If there is real rapport the alcoholic will very likely follow their suggestion. And if the alcoholic is wary of treatment, and resistant to A.A., the clergyman may suggest his going to an Alcoholism Information Center.

**Q. What is an Alcoholism Information Center?**

**A.** It is neutral ground, for one thing. Many people who will not enter what they consider the "cage" of treatment, since it means committing themselves to the idea that they *need* treatment, will go to a place called an Information Center, where they can find out what they want to know without committing themselves. In fact they usually come seeking information "for a friend." Primarily, an Alcoholism Information Center is the headquarters of a local Council on Alcoholism, out of which its public education program flows. Secondly, it is the place where anyone in the community can come to learn whatever he needs to know about the illness and what can be done about it. Its staff is well trained and eager to help. The Center does not give treatment, but it is fully informed on all available resources for help and makes referrals to them. In many cases a good referral may take several interviews at the Center, so that many of them have counselors on the staff. Some Centers hold classes for wives and husbands of alcoholics who are not yet ready to seek help themselves, and all of them will work with a wife or husband, devising a plan of action for their particular case. The national office and the eighty-odd Centers maintained by local Councils affiliated with the National Council on Alcoholism assisted nearly 200,000 alcoholics, families, and others concerned with alcoholics during 1968.

# 12. Treatment

**Q. Is there a specific treatment for alcoholism?**

**A.** No. It requires the knowledge of a specific cause to develop a specific treatment. Since we do not know the specific cause of alcoholism and since in any case it is generally agreed that there are many causes, it follows that there are many treatments.

**Q. Are these treatments alike or very different?**

**A.** They have one common denominator: they all try to help the alcoholic to stop drinking and to learn to live without alcohol. However, this common goal is approached in a wide variety of ways.

**Q. Is there any drug that will make the alcoholic stop drinking?**

**A.** No, there is no "magic pill," although alcoholics and their families would dearly like to find one. The nearest to it—and it is very far from this longed-for magic—is disulfiram (trade name: Antabuse). This is a drug which builds a "chemical fence" against drinking so long as it is in the system, and it remains in the system for five days after the individual stops taking it. There is no effect from the pill itself, *unless* the person drinks, and then there is a severe and most unpleasant reaction. Antabuse is immensely helpful to someone who really doesn't want to drink, but has trouble staying away from it. As one user said, "You only have to make one decision a day: to take the pill." It effectively stops impulsive drinking, and frees the alcoholic's mind from a constant preoccupation with whether or not to drink. However, there is nothing to prevent the alcoholic from stopping the Antabuse, waiting five days, and drinking as usual. So Antabuse alone is not treatment for alcoholism: it simply makes it possible to stay sober for a long enough period to benefit from treatment. It should also be emphasized that Antabuse must not be given to the alcoholic without his knowledge, since the reaction after drinking can be serious. If the alcoholic knows he has Antabuse in his system, he still might try a drink, but he would be very tentative about it, watching his own reaction carefully, and stopping as soon as he felt it. But if he doesn't know, he might well down two or three hefty drinks before he realizes what is happening, and the ambulance might have to be called quickly.

**Q. Are there other drugs that are used in treatment?**

**A.** Yes, quite a number. First it should be made clear that treatment is divided into two parts: (1) treatment of the acute phase, which is sobering up, or detoxification, and is wholly medical, and (2) treatment of the alcoholism itself, which is directed toward eliminating the chronic compulsion to drink. In the first case, hospitalization may be required, for people can die of acute alcoholism. Both sedatives and tranquilizers are used and often massive doses of vitamins. Initial medical treatments are numerous and very similar, and with the development of many new drugs this is no longer a difficult process and is accomplished in a few days. In treatment of the acute phase there is no question as to the value of both sedatives and tranquilizers. In treatment of the alcoholism itself, however, there is a big question as to the advisability of using either sedatives or tranquilizers since so many alcoholics are prone to addiction and are apt to use the drugs as a substitute for drinking, with even worse results. Most therapists in this field are exceedingly reluctant to give an alcoholic patient any drugs over the long course of treatment for the disease itself.

**Q. What is the best treatment for alcoholism?**

**A.** There is really no "best treatment," since all methods now in use have had success with some patients. What works with one may not work with another, so it is necessary to tailor the treatment to the particular patient's needs. The "treatment" that has worked for the greatest number of alcoholics is Alcoholics Anonymous.

**Q. Would you list these treatments?**

**A.** Alcoholics Anonymous, individual psychiatric treatment, multidisciplinary team treatment (as in an alcoholism clinic), counseling, group therapy, residential treatment. Within each of these there are variations in approach, in method, and in the use of adjuncts such as informational lectures, films, psychodrama, hypnosis, medication, relaxation techniques, etc.

**Q. What kind of treatment does Alcoholics Anonymous give?**

**A.** Treatment is not the right word for the A.A. program, yet it is listed above because of its proven success in bringing hundreds of thousands of alcoholics to recovery. It will be dealt with in Chapter 13.

**Q. How is psychiatric treatment used for alcoholism?**

**A.** In most cases just as it is used for other problems, with an effort to uncover root causes in the life and personality of the patient. The difficulty here is that classic psychiatry has tended to ignore what is too often described as "merely a symptom"—the drinking —on the theory that when the underlying causes are dealt with, the symptom will wither away. In alcoholism it just doesn't. The drinking seems to have a life of its own and must be dealt with first, before anything else can be done. Psychiatric treatment has been of the greatest use to alcoholics who have stopped drinking by other means and then sought help in learning how to identify and to manage their life problems without drinking.

**Q. Is psychoanalysis ever used?**

**A.** Rarely, and most analysts will not take an alcoholic. The analytic process is a painful one, and alcoholics are too apt to resort to their trusted pain-killer, alcohol, thus negating or hopelessly delaying the progress of treatment. Here again, psychoanalysis can be helpful in dealing with severe and deep-seated neurotic complications, after the alcoholic has been away from drinking for a considerable time.

**Q. What is multidisciplinary team treatment?**

**A.** Most alcoholism clinics and some residential treatment centers have staffs drawn from many disciplines, including psychiatrists, medical doctors, psychologists, psychiatric social workers, nurses, clergymen skilled in pastoral counseling, and trained lay counselors. Not all facilities use all of these, so there may be different combinations, and a medically oriented clinic might not use any of the psychiatrically trained disciplines. Most existing alcoholism clinics are psychiatrically oriented, and the bulk of the treatment work is carried out by social workers under the supervision of a psychiatrist. The patient, however, is seen by all members of the team, and each case is discussed by the entire team at regular staff meetings.

**Q. What is meant by counseling?**

**A.** I suspect that counseling has as many meanings as it has people doing it. One thing common to all counseling, however, is the ability to listen to the patient. In its highest sense, counseling means talking over the patient's problems with him, and guiding him to better ways of handling them. Pastoral counseling, of course, is spiritually based, and the effort is to bring the patient to a more spiritual approach to life through dealing with his immediate and very real problems.

**Q. What is group therapy?**

**A.** There are many forms of group therapy, but in general it is a small group of people who meet regularly with a leader, who may be a psychiatrist, a social worker, or a counselor, to discuss their problems. One of the great values is the close and regular contact with others who share the same problems and the group feeling which develops, encouraging the open discussion of deep and often long-hidden feelings. Many alcoholics learn for the first time that they are not unique and that their difficulties are no worse—and no different—from those of many others. This recognition is often the beginning of recovery.

**Q. Is alcoholism treated in state hospitals?**

**A.** Some state mental hospitals have excellent alcoholism services, while others do not accept alcoholics as such. It is necessary therefore to find out what the situation is at any particular state hospital.

**Q. What is residential treatment?**

**A.** In recent years there has been an upsurge in the number of residential treatment facilities which keep their patients an average of thirty days. They are called by a variety of names—treatment centers, rest homes, rehabilitation centers, recovery houses, halfway houses, etc.—and their methods of treatment are equally varied, with counseling predominant in all of them. A few of the best in the country, privately run, have developed treatment teams of clinical psychologists, clergymen, and trained lay counselors. Others are extremely informal, with the counseling done largely by the manager of the house. All of them work closely with Alcoholics Anonymous, either holding meetings on the premises or taking their patients to meetings, and many, in fact, are run by members of A.A. The best of them have shown themselves very effective, and this includes some of the most informally organized ones.

# 13. Alcoholics Anonymous

**Q. What is Alcoholics Anonymous?**

**A.** It is a loosely knit fellowship of men and women banded together to help solve their common problem of alcoholism, and dedicated to helping others who seek their help. It is made up of alcoholics, it works for alcoholics, by means of alcoholics, on a personal, face-to-face basis. It is not connected with any organization of any kind, nor does it sponsor or endorse any causes or activities such as treatment facilities or anything else. Its sole purpose is to help its members to stay sober and to help others to achieve sobriety.

**Q. Is A.A. a religious movement?**

**A.** No, it is not. It has no connection with any church, denomination, or creed. The fact that its twelve suggested steps to recovery have a spiritual base does not make it a religious group. Whenever the word God is used it is followed by the phrase "as you understand Him." This has enabled the A.A. program to be successfully utilized by people from all the world's great faiths—Buddhism, Christianity, Judaism, Muhammadanism, Shintoism—and also by agnostics and atheists.

**Q. Do people have to accept some spiritual belief before A.A. will help them?**

**A.** No. Many people come to A.A. with a strong resistance to any belief of any kind, and they are told that that is their own business—that no commitment is required of them. They are asked merely to listen, and to keep an open mind. I know one member whose resistance lasted for ten years, and no one ever questioned it. That member was able to stay sober all those years, and to help many others without ever imposing his own disbelief on them. Tolerance of others' beliefs and opinions is an important ingredient of the A.A. program.

**Q. How does A.A. help people?**

**A.** First of all, A.A. believes that alcoholics must seek their help. Its members do not go into bars, for instance, gathering up drunks. Nor will they call on an individual who has expressed no willingness to see them. But they will answer any alcoholic's call for help, and most communities have an A.A. Intergroup Office, which receives such calls and passes them on to a member who makes the return call. In smaller communities the group secretary's own number may be listed under Alcoholics Anonymous in the phone book, or the local number may be available from the local newspaper office or even from the police. In any case it is always possible to find an A.A. member to call.

**Q. Then what does that member do?**

**A.** If the person has called from home and is in bad shape, the A.A. member goes there and talks with him. He also listens. In fact, he may do much more listening than talking. The A.A. member has three things going for him. First, he is sober, clear-eyed, and healthy, looks as if he enjoyed being alive, and is well dressed. The alcoholic who has called from home usually looks like an unmade bed, is red-eyed and bleary, may be a little drunk or else is suffering from an appalling hangover, and feels so ill he wishes he were dead. He usually cannot believe that this contented, well man has ever felt the way he feels now. But the A.A. member can and does convince him that he has been in exactly the same spot many times. Therefore, second, the A.A. member knows exactly how the alcoholic feels, and his ability to convey this with a few well-chosen episodes out of his own drinking past easily convinces the sick alcoholic that here at last is someone who really understands—which is the truth. This allows the alcoholic to speak freely to the A.A. member, and a real conversation about his drinking problem becomes possible. Third, the A.A. member offers himself as an example of how the sick alcoholic can be if he stops drinking. He may say, "The difference between us is only one drink. If you *don't* take it you'll be like me. If I do take it I'll be like you." It's a very convincing argument.

**Q. Does it always happen that way?**

**A.** No. A great many people call at a time when they're sober, and they may make a date to meet an A.A. member somewhere. Or they may go to the Intergroup Office, where there are always a number of A.A. volunteers, there for the purpose of talking to new people who come in. Or a friend of the sick alcoholic who knows a member of A.A. may invite them both to dinner or lunch or to meet for coffee. Sometimes a doctor will send his patient to an A.A.-oriented treatment facility, and that may be the sick alcoholic's first contact with A.A. Or a doctor may put him in a general hospital's alcoholism unit, where members of A.A. visit. There are an infinite variety of ways in which a sick alcoholic may be brought in contact with a member of A.A.

**Q. What happens next?**

**A.** The new person is taken to a meeting as soon as possible. This is not just to hear what is being said at the meeting but also to meet other members of A.A.—to broaden his base, so to speak. It is conceivable that a real rapport might not have been established by the first A.A. member, or real grounds for a close relationship may not be apparent. But at a meeting the new person will have an opportunity to meet a large variety of people and to choose those he wants to know better. The new member is free to choose his own sponsor and may choose someone other than the first A.A. he met.

**Q. What is a sponsor?**

**A.** A sponsor is an established member with some solid sobriety behind him who is willing to take responsibility for the newcomer's start in the A.A. way of life. A sponsor will see the new member between meetings, will take him to meetings, or arrange to meet him there, and will answer his questions about the program. The relationship between a sponsor and his "pigeon" is one of the closest relationships known: it approximates the "buddy" relationship made famous in wartime.

**Q. What are these meetings?**

**A.** Meetings are of two kinds—open and closed. An open meeting is simply a gathering of A.A. members, newcomers, and often families and friends, to listen to talks by three or four members. The talks have a pattern: what it used to be like, how I found A.A., and what it's like now. Some of these "stories" are hilarious, some deeply serious, all of them very moving and uniformly fascinating. Since honesty is a basic part of the A.A. program, they are frank and revealing and of immense help to the newcomer in identifying with the speakers and with A.A. He often hears his own story from many different speakers, and the net result is that he is left in little doubt that he belongs there—that he has found "his own people." Closed meetings are for alcoholics only, and they are discussion meetings. There are a variety of formulas for these, but usually there is a leader who speaks for five or ten minutes, may or may not set a theme for the discussion, and then throws the meeting open for questions. Anyone present may answer, and sometimes everyone has something to contribute to the question. The questions are often about A.A. itself, more often about personal problems which may range far beyond drinking but usually have a bearing in the questioner's mind on whether he might drink. Following both kinds of meeting there is a coffee hour, often quite elaborate with cake and cookies, and always alive with conversation. Many A.A.s say that "this is when the real work gets done."

**Q. Is that all there is to A.A.?**

**A.** No. The basic program of A.A. is the "Twelve Suggested Steps." Sponsors, meetings, the 24-hour plan, and other A.A. practices are really techniques for helping people to follow the A.A. way of life.

**Q. What are the Twelve Steps?**

**A.**

1. We admitted we were powerless over alcohol—that our lives had become unmanageable.
2. Came to believe that a Power greater than ourselves could restore us to sanity.
3. Made a decision to turn our will and our lives over to the care of God, *as we understood Him.*
4. Made a searching and fearless moral inventory of ourselves.
5. Admitted to God, to ourselves, and to another human being the exact nature of our wrongs.
6. Were entirely ready to have God remove all these defects of character.
7. Humbly asked Him to remove our shortcomings.
8. Made a list of all persons we had harmed, and became willing to make amends to them all.
9. Made direct amends to such people wherever possible, except when to do so would injure them or others.
10. Continued to take personal inventory, and when we were wrong promptly admitted it.
11. Sought through prayer and meditation to improve our conscious contact with God *as we*

*understood Him*, praying only for knowledge of His will for us and the power to carry that out.

12. Having had a spiritual awakening as the result of these steps, we tried to carry this message to alcoholics, and to practice these principles in all our affairs.

**Q. How could agnostics or atheists accept those?**

**A.** Of course they don't—at first—or maybe for a long time. They aren't asked to. There are so many "techniques" that will help to keep them sober for a considerable time, that many just concentrate on those. Most agnostics and atheists, however, do believe in something—often the ethical man or the future of humanity, or social ideals. Such beliefs can act as their "Power greater than themselves." There have been some who considered the A.A. group that Power. One man chose a Fifth Avenue bus! Another chose electricity. These substitutes are usually temporary, and most A.A. members come to their own interpretation of God in due course.

**Q. What is the "24-hour plan"?**

**A.** Devised originally as a way of getting sober—one day at a time—and still used for that purpose (most A.A.s will tell you they are sober today; they make no guarantee for tomorrow), it came to be an effective way of dealing with many of life's problems. The philosophy is that all we have is today, tomorrow may never come, so go all out to do the best you can today, and if you do, tomorrow will take care of itself. If there is something you can do about a problem today, do it, otherwise forget it and concentrate on those things about which you can do something today. This works wonders for chronic worriers.

**Q. What does A.A. mean by "recovery"?**

**A.** First they mean sobriety, but they go further than that. They speak of the quality of sobriety and the responsible use of sobriety. In short, true recovery is thought to be a full reintegration into society, with responsible, efficient functioning and good interpersonal relationships—what they call "normal living."

**Q. Do people really recover for good in A.A.?**

**A.** Yes. This can be said because, after nearly thirty-five years of existence, many members have lived into their seventies and eighties and died sober and still active in A.A.

**Q. Do they have to go to meetings for the rest of their lives?**

**A.** No one *has* to do anything in A.A. It's entirely up to the individual. But experience has shown that those who continue active participation, which includes going to perhaps one meeting a week, stay sober, while those who drift away don't. The lesson seems obvious.

**Q. What is meant by an *active* member?**

**A.** Someone who attends meetings and takes part in voluntary activity, particularly what is called "twelfth step work," which means helping sick alcoholics, calling on them, and sponsoring them.

**Q. Does A.A. charge for its services?**

**A.** No. There are no dues or fees for joining or belonging to A.A., and no member makes a charge for his efforts. The small amounts of money needed for a group to function: the rent of a meeting place, money for coffee and cake, are raised by passing the basket at meetings. Just as many put in a dime as a dollar, and a broke newcomer is not expected to put in anything. A.A.'s international headquarters, the General Service Office, is supported by contributions from the groups and from individual members. No money is accepted from outsiders, individuals, foundations, or whatever. Even individual members are limited to not more than $200 a year. A.A. is self-supporting by means of its total membership.

**Q. What is their percentage of recovery?**

**A.** A.A. keeps no records on its members, so there is no hard figure. Observation would indicate that it is at least 50 per cent of those who had any contact whatever, which might mean just one meeting. This percentage may be going up with the recent trend toward younger people coming to A.A., who have not suffered so much damage or loss, and whose chances of recovery therefore are greater.

# 14.

# Al-Anon and Alateen

**Q. What is Al-Anon?**

**A.** The full name is Al-Anon Family Group, and these groups are made up of wives, husbands, relatives, and sometimes friends of alcoholics, banded together as in A.A. to help themselves and each other. They use the Twelve Steps of A.A., with minor adaptations, as their basic program, and they also use many of the techniques developed by A.A.—regular meetings, sponsorship, etc. Al-Anon is for the benefit of each nonalcoholic who goes there, *not* for his or her alcoholic, who has A.A. to go to. It is not a part of A.A., nor is it a place to talk about what their alcoholics did or are doing. It *is* a place for nonalcoholics to talk about themselves and their problems.

**Q. Why do they need help if they are not alcoholics?**

**A.** Alcoholism is unlike other diseases in that it adversely affects *everyone* in contact with the sufferer. The closer they are to him, the more adversely they are affected. The wife or husband of an alcoholic is in just as much trouble as the alcoholic, and needs help just as much, particularly if the alcoholic is still drinking. Too often they are totally ignorant about the illness or that it can be treated. They have a great need for sound information about it, for their own sake as well as for their alcoholic's. Frequently they bear a heavy and unnecessary burden of guilt, feeling they are somehow to blame for the drinking. Their alcoholic's behavior may have so isolated them from the normal world that they are an easy prey to loneliness and fear. In any case, they have found it impossible to help their alcoholic and are baffled, bewildered, and often deeply resentful, without knowing where to turn or what to do about it. In their ignorance, what they do is all too often the wrong thing, driving their alcoholic to greater drinking. What they learn from other Al-Anon members who have been through the same things, and what they gain from adopting the philosophy embodied in the Twelve Steps, can restore them to balance and inner comfort.

**Q. Is Al-Anon just for those whose alcoholics have not stopped drinking?**

A. No, it was started by wives and husbands of A.A. members. They found that they needed help in adjusting to the new situation. They also needed help in gaining full emotional acceptance of the fact that their alcoholic was suffering from an illness he had not sought and really did not want, that his behavior was symptomatic of this illness and did not mean that he did not love them or their children. This total acceptance is essential if they are to be really helpful to their alcoholic while he is trying to recover. Remember that recovery from alcoholism is a *process,* which takes time, and requires patience and understanding cooperation. If they cannot give this, their alcoholic might not make it.

**Q. But they do help those whose alcoholics are still drinking?**

A. Yes, and many wives and husbands have found that their participation in Al-Anon has helped them so much in managing their own lives despite their alcoholic's disruptive behavior, that they have become quite changed people. This change in them often brings changes in the alcoholic, and he becomes ready to accept help.

**Q. What is Alateen?**

**A.** This is a similar fellowship for the teen-age children of alcoholics and does the same kind of thing for them. One of the most tragic effects of alcoholism is what it does to the children, who are far from unaware of the situation. The shame they feel can be overwhelming, and it often escalates into resentment and a deep anger—not just at the alcoholic but at the whole world. For instance, a good deal of juvenile delinquency can be traced to an alcoholic parent, as can school problem-children. They too can become isolated and withdrawn. For these children Alateen offers understanding of their parents' illness, companionship with others who have a similar situation, and, most of all, a new way of living and thinking—the A.A. way of life.

**Q. Do the children run these groups themselves?**

**A.** Each group has an advisor, usually a member of Al-Anon. Alateen meetings too are patterned on A.A. meetings.

**Q. How can you find Al-Anon or Alateen?**

**A.** They may be listed in the phone book; if not, the local A.A. group, which almost always has a telephone listing, can tell you.

# Bibliography

Available at bookstores, from the publisher, or from the National Council on Alcoholism, 733 Third Avenue, New York, New York 10017.


Alcoholics Anonymous. *Alcoholics Anonymous.* 2nd ed. New York: Alcoholics Anonymous World Services, Inc., 1955.

Almond, R. *The Healing Community.* New York: Jason Aronson, 1974.

Block, Marvin A., M.D. *Alcoholism, Its Facets and Phases.* New York: John Day Co., 1962.

Criteria Committee, National Council on Alcoholism. *American Journal of Psychiatry,* 1972.

Estes, Nada J., and Heinemann, M. Edith. *Alcoholism: Development, Consequences and Interventions.* St. Louis, Missouri: C. V. Mosby Co., 1977.

Ewing, John A., and Rouse, Beatrice A. *Drinking–Alcohol in American Society–Issues and Current Research.* Chicago: Nelson Hall, 1978.

Fajardo, Roque. *Helping Your Alcoholic Before He or She Hits Bottom.* New York: Crown Publishers, 1976.

Filstead, William J., Ph.D., Rossi, Jean J., Ph.D., and Keller, Mark. *Alcohol and Alcohol Problems: New Thinking and New Directions.* Cambridge, Massachusetts: Ballinger Publishing Co., 1976.

Fox, Ruth, M.D., and Lyon, Peter. *Alcoholism, Its Scope, Cause, and Treatment.* New York: Random House, 1955.

Hancock, D. C. *I Can't Be an Alcoholic Because . . . .* Lansing, Michigan: Michigan Alcohol and Drug Information Center, 1969.

Heilman, R. O. "Dynamics of Drug Dependency." *Minnesota Medicine,* 1973.

Heilman, R. O. *Early Recognition of Alcoholism and Other Drug Dependence.* Center City, Minnesota: Hazelden Foundation.

Jellinek, Dr. E. M. *The Alcoholism Complex.* Mill Neck, New York: Christopher D. Smithers Foundation, Inc., rev. 1976.

Jellinek, Dr. E. M. "Phases of Alcohol Addiction." *Quarterly Journal of Studies on Alcohol,* 1952.

Johnson, V. E. *I'll Quit Tomorrow.* New York: Harper & Row, 1973.

Keller, J. E. *Ministering to Alcoholics.* Minneapolis: Augsburg Publishing House, 1966.

McAuliffe, R. M., and McAuliffe, M. B. *The Essentials of Chemical Dependency.* Chanhassen, Minnesota: The American Chemical Dependency Center, 1975.

Maxwell, Ruth. *The Booze Battle.* New York: Praeger Publishers, 1976.

Milt, Harry. *Alcoholics and Alcoholism.* Public Affairs Pamphlet No. 426, 1967.

Silverstein, Dr. Alvin, and Silverstein, Virginia B. *Alcoholism.* New York: J. B. Lippincott Company, 1975.

Smithers, Christopher D. *Understanding Alcoholism: for the Patient, the Family and the Employer.* New York: Charles Scribner's Sons, 1968.

Strachan, George J. *Alcoholism: Treatable Illness.* Vancouver: Mitchell Press Ltd., 1968.

Tiebout, H. M. *Direct Treatment of a Symptom.* Center City, Minnesota: Hazelden Foundation.

Tiebout, H. M. *Intervention in Psychotherapy.* Center City, Minnesota: Hazelden Foundation, (Reprinted from *The American Journal of Psychoanalysis,* 1962).

Weiner, Jack B. *Drinking.* New York: W. W. Norton Co., 1976.

## ABOUT THE AUTHOR . . . .

Marty Mann was the daughter of a Chicago department store executive. When she returned from a European education in 1926, America was in the midst of Prohibition. Not realizing that alcohol was physically dangerous to her, she fell into the then fashionable habit of visiting speakeasies. Her problem with drinking worsened over the years, and in 1939 she had to enter a sanitarium. At the time, no hospital would accept an acutely sick alcoholic; there were few outpatient clinics, no special alcoholism units in state hospitals, and no halfway or recovery houses for alcoholics. But there was Alcoholics Anonymous, and Marty Mann was the first woman to join, though even here she met resistance from people who believed that women could not suffer from the disease of alcoholism. By 1944, her recovery complete, Marty Mann concluded that some vast and special effort was needed to bring the kind of knowledge that had saved her life to everyone. With the backing of a group of scientists at Yale University working on the problem of alcoholism, she founded the National Council on Alcoholism and became its first Executive Director. NCA's major purpose was to teach the public the facts about alcoholism and what could be done about it, hoping to change public attitudes from negative apathy to positive action. From this forum she worked tirelessly to bring hope to alcoholics around the world, giving over 200 lectures every year and acting as a consultant to state alcohol programs, state and city health departments, and the United States Public Health Service. Marty Mann was also a consultant to the National Institute of Alcohol Abuse and Alcoholism in Washington as well as a fellow of the Royal Society of Health in London.

## Also by Don DeLillo

**NOVELS**

Americana

End Zone

Great Jones Street

Ratner's Star

Players

Running Dog

The Names

White Noise

Libra

Mao II

Underworld

**PLAYS**

The Day Room

Valparaiso

# THE BODY ARTIST

A NOVEL

DON DeLILLO

SCRIBNER

NEW YORK LONDON TORONTO SYDNEY SINGAPORE

SCRIBNER
1230 Avenue of the Americas
New York, NY 10020



DESIGNED BY ERICH HOBBING

Set in Electra

Manufactured in the United States of America

1 3 5 7 9 10 8 6 4 2

Library of Congress Cataloging-in-Publication Data
DeLillo, Don.
The body artist : a novel / Don DeLillo.
p. cm.
I.Title.
PS3554.E4425 B63 2001
813'.54—dc21 00-058842

ISBN 0-7432-0395-X

# THE BODY ARTIST

## CHAPTER 1

Time seems to pass. The world happens, unrolling into moments, and you stop to glance at a spider pressed to its web. There is a quickness of light and a sense of things outlined precisely and streaks of running luster on the bay. You know more surely who you are on a strong bright day after a storm when the smallest falling leaf is stabbed with self-awareness. The wind makes a sound in the pines and the world comes into being, irreversibly, and the spider rides the wind-swayed web.

It happened this final morning that they were here at the same time, in the kitchen, and they shambled past each other to get things out of cabinets and drawers and then waited one for the other by the sink or fridge, still a little puddled in dream melt, and she ran tap water over the blueberries bunched in her hand and closed her eyes to breathe the savor rising.

He sat with the newspaper, stirring his coffee. It was

his coffee and his cup. They shared the newspaper but it was actually, unspokenly, hers.

"I want to say something but what."

She ran water from the tap and seemed to notice. It was the first time she'd ever noticed this.

"About the house. This is what it is," he said. "Something I meant to tell you."

She noticed how water from the tap turned opaque in seconds. It ran silvery and clear and then in seconds turned opaque and how curious it seemed that in all these months and all these times in which she'd run water from the kitchen tap she'd never noticed how the water ran clear at first and then went not murky exactly but opaque, or maybe it hadn't happened before, or she'd noticed and forgotten.

She crossed to the cabinet with the blueberries wet in her hand and reached up for the cereal and took the box to the counter, the mostly brown and white box, and then the toaster thing popped and she flipped it down again because it took two flips to get the bread to go brown and he absently nodded his acknowledgment because it was his toast and his butter and then he turned on the radio and got the weather.

The sparrows were at the feeder, wing-beating, fighting for space on the curved perches.

She reached into the near cabinet for a bowl and shook some cereal out of the box and then dropped the berries on top. She rubbed her hand dry on her jeans, feeling a sense somewhere of the color blue, runny and wan.

What's it called, the lever. She'd pressed down the lever to get his bread to go brown.

It was his toast, it was her weather. She listened to reports and called the weather number frequently and sometimes stood out front and looked into the coastal sky, tasting the breeze for latent implications.

"Yes exactly. I know what it is," he said.

She went to the fridge and opened the door. She stood there remembering something.

She said, "What?" Meaning what did you say, not what did you want to tell me.

She remembered the soya granules. She crossed to the cabinet and took down the box and then caught the fridge door before it swung shut. She reached in for the milk, realizing what it was he'd said that she hadn't heard about eight seconds ago.

Every time she had to bend and reach into the lower and remote parts of the refrigerator she let out a groan, but not really every time, that resembled a life lament. She was too trim and limber to feel the strain and was only echoing Rey, identifyingly, groaning his groan, but in a manner so seamless and deep it was her discomfort too.

Now that he'd remembered what he meant to tell her, he seemed to lose interest. She didn't have to see his face to know this. It was in the air. It was in the pause that trailed from his remark of eight, ten, twelve seconds ago. Something insignificant. He would take it as a kind of self-diminishment, bringing up a matter so trivial.

She went to the counter and poured soya over the cereal and fruit. The lever sprang or sprung and he got up and took his toast back to the table and then went for the butter and she had to lean away from the counter when he approached, her milk carton poised, so he could open the drawer and get a butter knife.

There were voices on the radio in like Hindi it sounded.

She poured milk into the bowl. He sat down and got up. He went to the fridge and got the orange juice and stood in the middle of the room shaking the carton to float the pulp and make the juice thicker. He never remembered the juice until the toast was done. Then he shook the carton. Then he poured the juice and watched a skim of sizzling foam appear at the top of the glass.

She picked a hair out of her mouth. She stood at the counter looking at it, a short pale strand that wasn't hers and wasn't his.

He stood shaking the container. He shook it longer than he had to because he wasn't paying attention, she thought, and because it was satisfying in some dumb and blameless way, for its own childlike sake, for the bounce and slosh and cardboard orange aroma.

He said, "Do you want some of this?"

She was looking at the hair.

"Tell me because I'm not sure. Do you drink juice?" he said, still shaking the damn thing, two fingers pincered at the spout.

She scraped her upper teeth over her tongue to rid her system of the complicated sense memory of someone else's hair.

She said, "What? Never drink the stuff. You know that. How long have we been living together?"

"Not long," he said.

He got a glass, poured the juice and watched the foam appear. Then he wheeled a little achingly into his chair.

"Not long enough for me to notice the details," he said.

"I always think this isn't supposed to happen here. I think anywhere but here."

He said, "What?"

"A hair in my mouth. From someone else's head."

He buttered his toast.

"Do you think it only happens in big cities with mixed populations?"

"Anywhere but here." She held the strand of hair between thumb and index finger, regarding it with mock aversion, or real aversion stretched to artistic limits, her mouth at a palsied slant. "That's what I think."

"Maybe you've been carrying it since childhood." He went back to the newspaper. "Did you have a pet dog?"

"Hey. What woke *you* up?" she said.

It was her newspaper. The telephone was his except when she was calling the weather. They both used the computer but it was spiritually hers.

She stood at the counter looking at the hair. Then she snapped it off her fingers to the floor. She turned to the sink and ran hot water over her hand and then took the cereal bowl to the table. Birds scattered when she moved near the window.

"I've seen you drink gallons of juice, tremendous, how can I tell you?" he said.

Her mouth was still twisted from the experience of sharing some food handler's unknown life or from a reality far stranger and more meandering, the intimate passage of the hair from person to person and somehow mouth to mouth across years and cities and diseases and unclean foods and many baneful body fluids.

"What? I don't think so," she said.

Okay, she put the bowl on the table. She went to the stove, got the kettle and filled it from the tap. He changed stations on the radio and said something she missed. She took the kettle back to the stove because this is how you live a life even if you don't know it and then she scraped her teeth over her tongue again, for emphasis, watching the flame shoot blue from the burner.

She'd had to sort of jackknife away from the counter when he approached to get the butter knife.

She moved toward the table and the birds went cracking off the feeder again. They passed out of the shade beneath the eaves and flew into sunglare and silence and it was an action she only partly saw, elusive and mutely beautiful, the birds so sunstruck they were consumed by light, disembodied, turned into something sheer and fleet and scatter-bright.

She sat down and picked through sections of newspaper and realized she had no spoon. She had no spoon. She looked at him and saw he was sporting a band-aid at the side of his jaw.

She used the old dented kettle instead of the new one she'd just bought because—she didn't know why. It was an old frame house that had many rooms and working fireplaces and animals in the walls and mildew everywhere, a place they'd rented unseen, a relic of the boom years of the lumbering and shipbuilding trades, way too big, and there were creaking floorboards and a number of bent utensils dating to god knows.

She half fell out of her chair in a gesture of self-ridicule and went to the counter to get a spoon. She took the soya granules back to the table as well. The soya had a smell that didn't seem to belong to the sandy stuff in the box. It was a faint wheaty stink with feet mixed in. Every time she used the soya she smelled it. She smelled it two or three times.

"Cut yourself again."

"What?" He put his hand to his jaw, head sunk in the newspaper. "Just a nick."

She started to read a story in her part of the paper. It

was an old newspaper, Sunday's, from town, because there were no deliveries here.

"That's lately, I don't know, maybe you shouldn't shave first thing. Wake up first. Why shave at all? Let your mustache grow back. Grow a beard."

"Why shave at all? There must be a reason," he said. "I want God to see my face."

He looked up from the paper and laughed in the empty way she didn't like. She took a bite of cereal and looked at another story. She tended lately to place herself, to insert herself into certain stories in the newspaper. Some kind of daydream variation. She did it and then became aware she was doing it and then sometimes did it again a few minutes later with the same or a different story and then became aware again.

She reached for the soya box without looking up from the paper and poured some granules into the bowl and the radio played traffic and talk.

The idea seemed to be that she'd have to wear out the old kettle, use it and use it until it developed rust bubbles and then and only then would it be okay for her to switch to the kettle she'd just bought.

"Do you have to listen to the radio?"

"No," she said and read the paper. "What?"

"It is such astonishing shit."

The way he stressed the *t* in shit, dignifying the word.

"I didn't turn on the radio. You turned on the radio," she said.

He went to the fridge and came back with a large dark fig and turned off the radio.

"Give me some of that," she said, reading the paper.

"I was not blaming. Who turned it on, who turned it off. Someone's a little edgy this morning. I'm the one, what do I say, who should be defensive. Not the young woman who eats and sleeps and lives forever."

"What? Hey, Rey. Shut up."

He bit off the stem and tossed it toward the sink. Then he split the fig open with his thumbnails and took the spoon out of her hand and licked it off and used it to scoop a measure of claret flesh out of the gaping fig skin. He dropped this stuff on his toast—the flesh, the mash, the pulp—and then spread it with the bottom of the spoon, blood-buttery swirls that popped with seedlife.

"I'm the one to be touchy in the morning. I'm the one to moan. The terror of another ordinary day," he said slyly. "You don't know this yet."

"Give us all a break," she told him.

She leaned forward, he extended the bread. There were crows in the trees near the house, taking up a raucous call. She took a bite and closed her eyes so she could think about the taste.

He gave back her spoon. Then he turned on the radio and remembered he'd just turned it off and he turned it off again.

She poured granules into the bowl. The smell of the soya was somewhere between body odor, yes, in the lower extremities and some authentic podlife of the earth, deep and seeded. But that didn't describe it. She read a story in the paper about a child abandoned in some godforsaken. Nothing described it. It was pure smell. It was the thing that smell is, apart from all sources. It was as though and she nearly said something to this effect because it might amuse him but then she let it drop—it was as though some, maybe, medieval scholastic had attempted to classify all known odors and had found something that did not fit into his system and had called it soya, which could easily be part of a lofty Latin term, but no it couldn't, and she sat thinking of something, she wasn't sure what, with the spoon an inch from her mouth.

He said, "What?"

"I didn't say anything."

She got up to get something. She looked at the kettle and realized that wasn't it. She knew it would come to her because it always did and then it did. She wanted honey for her tea even though the water wasn't boiling yet. She had a hyper-preparedness, or haywire, or hair-trigger, and Rey was always saying, or said once, and she carried a voice in her head that was hers and it was dialogue or monologue and she went to the cabinet where she got the honey and the tea bags—a voice that flowed from a story in the paper.

"Weren't you going to tell me something?"

He said, "What?"

She put a hand on his shoulder and moved past to her side of the table. The birds broke off the feeder in a wing-whir that was all *b*'s and *r*'s, the letter *b* followed by a series of vibrato *r*'s. But that wasn't it at all. That wasn't anything like it.

"You said something. I don't know. The house."

"It's not interesting. Forget it."

"I don't want to forget it."

"It's not interesting. Let me put it another way. It's boring."

"Tell me anyway."

"It's too early. It's an effort. It's boring."

"You're sitting there talking. Tell me," she said.

She took a bite of cereal and read the paper.

"It's an effort. It's like what. It's like pushing a boulder."

"You're sitting there talking."

"Here," he said.

"You said the house. Nothing about the house is boring. I like the house."

"You like everything. You love everything. You're my happy home. Here," he said.

He handed her what remained of his toast and she chewed it mingled with cereal and berries. Suddenly she knew what he'd meant to tell her. She heard the crows in large numbers now, clamorous in the trees, probably mobbing a hawk.

"Just tell me. Takes only a second," she said, knowing absolutely what it was.

She saw him move his hand to his breast pocket and then pause and lower it to the cup. It was his coffee, his cup and his cigarette. How an incident described in the paper seemed to rise out of the inky lines of print and gather her into it. You separate the Sunday sections.

"Just tell me okay. Because I know anyway."

He said, "What? You insist you will drag this thing out of me. Lucky we don't normally have breakfast together. Because my mornings."

"I know anyway. So tell me."

He was looking at the paper.

"You know. Then fine. I don't have to tell you."

He was reading, getting ready to go for his cigarettes.

She said, "The noise."

He looked at her. He looked. Then he gave her the great smile, the gold teeth in the great olive-dark face. She hadn't seen this in a while, the amplified smile, Rey emergent, his eyes clear and lit, deep lines etched about his mouth.

"The noises in the walls. Yes. You've read my mind."

"It was one noise. It was one noise," she said. "And it wasn't in the walls."

"One noise. Okay. I haven't heard it lately. This is what I wanted to say. It's gone. Finished. End of conversation."

"True. Except I heard it yesterday, I think."

"Then it's not gone. Good. I'm happy for you."

"It's an old house. There's always a noise. But this is different. Not those damn scampering animals we hear at night. Or the house settling. I don't know," she said, not wanting to sound concerned. "Like there's something."

She read the paper, voice trailing off.

"Good. I'm glad," he said. "You need the company."

You separate the Sunday sections and there are endless identical lines of print with people living somewhere in the words and the strange contained reality of paper and ink seeps through the house for a week and when you look at a page and distinguish one line from another it begins to gather you into it and there are people being tortured halfway around the world, who speak another language, and you have conversations with them more or less uncontrollably until you become aware you are doing it and then you stop, seeing whatever is in front of you at the time, like half a glass of juice in your husband's hand.

She took a bite of cereal and forgot to taste it. She lost the taste somewhere between the time she put the food in her mouth and the regretful second she swallowed it.

He put down the juice glass. He took the pack out of his shirt and lit up a cigarette, the cigarette he'd been smoking with his coffee since he was twelve years old, he'd told her, and he let the match burn down a bit before he shook it out in meditative slow motion and put it at the edge of his plate. It was agreeable to her, the smell of tobacco. It was part of her knowledge of his body. It was the aura of the man, a residue of smoke and unbroken habit, a dimension in the night, and she lapped it off the curled gray hairs on his chest and tasted it in his mouth. It was who he was in the dark, cigarettes and mumbled sleep and a hundred other things nameable and not.

But it wasn't one of his, the hair she'd found in her mouth. Employees must wash hands before leaving toilet. It was his toast but she'd eaten nearly half of it. It was his coffee and cup. Touch his cup and he looks at you edgewise, with the formal one-eyed glare of a boxer touching gloves. But she knew she was making this up because he didn't give a damn what you did with his cup. There were plenty of cups he could use. The phone was his. The birds were hers, the sparrows pecking at sunflower seeds. The hair was somebody else's.

He said something about his car, the mileage, gesturing. He liked to conduct, to guide an extended remark with his hand, a couple of fingers jutting.

"All day yesterday I thought it was Friday."

He said, "What?"

Or you become someone else, one of the people in the story, doing dialogue of your own devising. You become a man at times, living between the lines, doing another version of the story.

She thought and read. She groped for the soya box and her hand struck the juice container. She looked up and understood he wasn't reading the paper. He was looking at it but not reading it and she understood this retroactively, that he'd been looking at it all this time but not absorbing the words on the page.

The container remained upright. She poured a little more soya into the bowl, for grainy texture and long life.

"All day yesterday I thought it was Friday."

He said, "Was it?"

She remembered to smile.

He said, "What does it matter anyway?"

She'd put a hand on his shoulder and then nearly moved it up along the back of his neck and into his hair, caressingly, but hadn't.

"I'm only saying. How does it happen that Thursday seems like Friday? We're out of the city. We're off the calendar. Friday shouldn't have an identity here. Who wants more coffee?"

She went to pour water for her tea and paused at the stove, waiting for him to say yes or no to coffee. When she started back she saw a blue jay perched atop the feeder. She stopped dead and held her breath. It stood large and polished and looked royally remote from the other birds busy feeding and she could nearly believe she'd never seen a jay before. It stood enormous, looking in at her, seeing whatever it saw, and she wanted to tell Rey to look up.

She watched it, black-barred across the wings and tail, and she thought she'd somehow only now learned how to look. She'd never seen a thing so clearly and it was not simply because the jay was posted where it was, close enough for her to note the details of cresting and color. There was also the clean shock of its appearance among the smaller brownish birds, its mineral blue and muted blue and broad dark neckband. But if Rey looked up, the bird would fly.

She tried to work past the details to the bird itself, nest thief and skilled mimic, to the fixed interest in those eyes, a kind of inquisitive chill that felt a little like a challenge.

When birds look into houses, what impossible worlds they see. Think. What a shedding of every knowable surface and process. She wanted to believe the bird was seeing her, a woman with a teacup in her hand, and never mind the folding back of day and night, the apparition of a space set off from time. She looked and took a careful breath. She was alert to the clarity of the moment but knew it was ending already. She felt it in the blue jay. Or maybe not. She was making it happen herself because she could not look any longer. This must be what it means to see if you've been near blind all your life. She said something to Rey, who lifted his head slightly, chasing the jay but leaving the sparrows unstartled.

"Did you see it?"

He half turned to answer.

"Don't we see them all the time?"

"Not all the time. And never so close."

"Never so close. Okay."

"It was looking at me."

"It was looking at you."

She was standing in place, off his left shoulder. When she moved toward her chair the sparrows flew.

"It was watching me."

"Did it make your day?"

"It made my day. My week. What else?"

She drank her tea and read. Nearly everything she read sent her into reverie.

She turned on the radio and tracked slowly along the dial, reading the paper, trying to find the weather on the radio.

He finished his coffee and smoked.

She sat over the bowl of cereal. She looked past the bowl into a space inside her head that was also here in front of her.

She folded a section of newspaper and read a line or two and read some more or didn't, sipping tea and drifting.

The radio reported news about a missile exploding mysteriously, underground, in Montana, and she didn't catch if it was armed or not.

He smoked and looked out the window to his right, where an untended meadow tumbled to the rutted dirt road that led to a gravel road.

She read and drifted. She was here and there.

The tea had no honey in it. She'd left the honey jar unopened by the stove.

He looked around for an ashtray.

She had a conversation with a doctor in a news story.

There were two miles of gravel before you reached the paved road that led to town.

She took the fig off his plate and put a finger down into it and reamed around inside for flesh.

A voice reported the weather but she missed it. She didn't know it was the weather until it was gone.

He eased his head well back and rolled it slowly side to side to lessen the tension in his neck.

She sucked the finger on her fig-dipping hand and thought of things they needed from the store.

He turned off the radio.

She sipped her tea and read. She more or less saw herself talking to a doctor in the bush somewhere, with people hungry in the dust.

The cigarette was burning down in his hand.

She picked up the soya box and tipped it toward her face and smelled inside.

When he walked out of the room, she realized there was something she wanted to tell him.

Sometimes she doesn't think of what she wants to say to him until he walks out of whatever room they're in. Then she thinks of it. Then she either calls after him or doesn't and he responds or doesn't.

She sat there and finished her tea and thought of what she thought of, memory traces and flary images and a friend she missed and all the shadow-dappled stuff of an undividable moment on a normal morning going crazy in ways so humanly routine you can't even stop and take note except for the Ajax she needs to buy and the birds behind her, rattling the metal frame of the feeder.

It's such a stupid thing to do, read the newspaper and eat.

She saw him standing in the doorway.

"Have you seen my keys?"

She said, "What?"

He waited for the question to register.

"Which keys?" she said.

He looked at her.

She said, "I bought some lotion yesterday. Which I meant to tell you. It's a muscle rub. It's in a green and white tube on the shelf in the big bathroom upstairs. It's greaseless. It's a muscle rub. Rub it in, my love. Or ask me nice, I'll do it for you."

"All my keys are on one ring," he said.

She almost said, Is that smart? But then she didn't. Because what a needless thing. Because how petty it would be to say such a thing, in the morning or any time, on a strong bright day after a storm.

## REY ROBLES, 64,
## CINEMA'S POET OF LONELY PLACES

Rey Robles, who directed two world-renowned movies of the late 1970s, was found dead Sunday morning in the Manhattan apartment of his first wife, the fashion consultant Isabel Corrales.

The cause of death was a self-inflicted gunshot wound, according to police who were called to the scene.

Mr. Robles's accounts of his early life were inconsistent but the most persuasive independent versions suggest he was 64 at his death.

He was born Alejandro Alquezar, in Barcelona. A biographical sketch in the journal *Cahiers du Cinéma* asserted that his father, a worker in a textile plant and a militant antifascist, was killed in that city during the fiercest street fighting of the civil war. The article cites evidence that Alejandro, still a small boy, was among the "war children" of Spain who were sent to the Soviet Union by their families when the dictatorship of the right became an impending reality.

It isn't clear how many years he spent in the USSR or whether he was ever reunited with his mother. It is known that he lived in Paris as a young man, hauling trash, performing as a street juggler and playing bit parts in several movies, cast as a thief or pimp. This is when he adopted the name Rey Robles, after a minor character he played in an obscure film noir.

He spent a few years in New York writing subtitles for a trickle of Spanish-language and Russian films and then went west, finding work as a uniformed chauffeur in Los Angeles, where he continued a fringe relationship with the movies, appearing as an extra in half a dozen films. He got a start on the other side of the camera after he became the personal driver of a multimillionaire cement manufacturer from Liechtenstein, a man who was a heavy investor in international film projects. By his own account, Mr. Robles had an affair with the man's wife and persuaded her to arrange a job for him as a second-unit director on a spaghetti western scheduled to be shot in Spain.

Ten years later, at the Cannes Film Festival, Mr. Robles told an appreciative audience, "The answer to life is the movies."

He directed eight features in all. The third of these, *My Life for Yours,* a French-Italian co-production about a wealthy woman kidnapped by Corsican bandits, won the Palme d'Or at Cannes. It was followed by *Polaris,* a tense American crime drama with an undercurrent of Spanish surrealism. The film developed a cult following and ran for extended periods in a number of art houses in this country and abroad.

"His work at its best extends the language of film," wrote the critic Philip Stansky. "His subject is people in landscapes of estrangement. He found a spiritual knife-edge in the poetry of alien places, where extreme situations become inevitable and characters are forced toward life-defining moments."

His subsequent movies failed commercially and were largely dismissed by critics. Friends of Mr. Robles attribute his decline to alcoholism and intermittent depression. He married the stage actress Anna Langdon during this period. They separated shortly afterward amid lurid headlines in the British tabloids and were eventually divorced.

He is survived by his third wife, Lauren Hartke, the body artist.

## CHAPTER 2

It's a hazy white day and the highway lifts to a drained sky. There are four northbound lanes and you are driving in the third lane and there are cars ahead and behind and to both sides, although not too many and not too close. When you reach the top of the incline, something happens and the cars begin to move unhurriedly now, seemingly self-propelled, coasting smoothly on the level surface. Everything is slow and hazy and drained and it all happens around the word *seem*. All the cars including yours seem to flow in dissociated motion, giving the impression of or presenting the appearance of, and the highway runs in a white hum.

Then the mood passes. The noise and rush and blur are back and you slide into your life again, feeling the painful weight in your chest.

She thought of these days as the first days back.

In the first days back she restocked the pantry and

sprayed chemicals on the bathroom tile. There was a full-size pantry, a dark musty room off the kitchen, and it didn't need restocking. She cleaned and filled the bird feeders, shaping the day around a major thing with all its wrinkles and twists, its array of swarming variations. She sprayed the tile and porcelain with pine-scent chemicals, half addicted to the fumes. There were two months left on the rental agreement. They'd rented for six and now there were two. One person, two months. She used a bottle with a pistol-grip attachment.

It felt like home, being here, and she raced through the days with their small ravishing routines, days the same, paced and organized but with a simultaneous wallow, uncentered, sometimes blank in places, days that moved so slow they ached.

She looked at the pages she'd been working on with Rey, his bullshit autobiography. The hard copy sat there, stark against her sense of his spoken recollections, the tapestried lies and contrivances, stories shaped out of desperations not always clear to her. She hand-patted through the clothes he'd left in the bedroom closet. She was not undone by the things that people leave behind when they die and she put the clothes in a box for the needy.

When she was downstairs she felt him in the rooms on the second floor. He used to prowl these rooms talking into a tiny tape recorder, smoke in his face, reciting ideas about some weary script to a writer somewhere whose name he could never recall. Now he was the smoke, Rey was, the thing in the air, vaporous, drifting into every space sooner or later, unshaped, but with a face that was somehow part of the presence, specific to the prowling man.

She climbed the stairs, hearing the sound a person makes who is climbing stairs, and she touched the oak grain of the newel when she reached the landing.

It was okay. She wanted to be here and she'd be okay. All their marriage, all the time they'd lived together they'd lived right here.

Her body felt different to her in ways she did not understand. Tight, framed, she didn't know exactly. Slightly foreign and unfamiliar. Different, thinner, didn't matter.

There was a package of bread crumbs on one of the shelves in the pantry. She knew she'd seen wax paper somewhere in a blue and something box. These were the things that were important now. Meals, tasks, errands.

She stepped slowly through the rooms. She felt him behind her when she was getting undressed, standing barefoot on the cold floor, throwing off a grubby sweater, and she half turned toward the bed.

In the first days back she got out of the car once and nearly collapsed—not the major breakdown of every significant function but a small helpless sinking toward the ground, a kind of forgetting how to stand.

She thought about broiling a cutlet, self-consciously

alone, more or less seeing herself from the edge of the room or standing precisely where she was and being who she was and seeing a smaller hovering her in the air somewhere, already thinking it's tomorrow.

She wanted to disappear in Rey's smoke, be dead, be him, and she tore the wax paper along the serrated edge of the box and reached for the carton of bread crumbs.

When the phone rang she did not look at it the way they do in the movies. Real people don't look at ringing phones.

The wax paper separated from the roll in rat-a-tat sequence, advancing along the notched edge of the box, and she heard it along her spine, she thought.

She was always thinking into tomorrow. She planned the days in advance. She sat in the panelled room. She stood in the tub and sprayed high on the tile walls until the depraved pine reek of acid and ether began to overwhelm her. It was hard to stop pressing the trigger.

She burned her hand on the skillet and went right to the fridge and there was no ice in the fucking. She hadn't filled the fucking ice thing.

People pick up ringing phones or don't. She listened to it ring. It sounded through the house, all the handsets jingling in their cradles.

How completely strange it suddenly seemed that major corporations mass-produced bread crumbs and packaged and sold them everywhere in the world and she looked at the bread-crumb carton for the first true time, really seeing it and understanding what was in it, and it was bread crumbs.

She sat in the panelled room and tried to read. First she'd build a fire. It was a room designed aspiringly for a brandy and a fire, a failed room, perversely furnished, and she drank tea and tried to read a book. But she'd make her way through a page and stare indifferently at objects fixed in space.

In the first days back she ate a clam from hell and spent a number of subsequent hours scuttling to the toilet. But at least she had her body back. There's nothing like a raging crap, she thought, to make mind and body one.

She climbed the stairs, hearing herself from other parts of the house somehow.

She threw off a grubby sweater. She raised her arm out of the sweater and struck her hand lightly on something above, wondering what it was, although this had happened before, and then she remembered the hanging lamp, metal shade wobbling, the lamp that was totally wrong for the room, and she turned toward the bed and looked, half looked, not looked in expectation but something else—a meaning so thin she could not read it.

There were too many things to understand and finally just one.

In town she saw a white-haired woman, Japanese, alone on a stone path in front of her house. She held a garden hose and stood weightless under lowering skies, so flat and still she might be gift wrap, and she watered a border of scarlet phlox, a soft spray arching from the nozzle.

Things she saw seemed doubtful—not doubtful but ever changing, plunged into metamorphosis, something that is also something else, but what, and what.

She began to pick up the phone. She used a soft voice at first, not quite her own, a twisted tentative other's voice, to say hello, who is this, yes. Word had gotten around that she was here and the calls were from New York, where she lived, and from friends and colleagues in other cities. They called from the cities to tell her they didn't understand why she'd come back here. It was the last place she ought to be, alone in a large house on an empty coast, and she stepped through the rooms and climbed the stairs and planned the days in advance because there was more to do in less time as the light grew threatened. You looked and it was dark, always unexpected.

She woke early every morning and this was the worst time, the first murderous instant of lying in bed and remembering something and knowing in the flow of the same breath what it was.

They called five or six times a day and then a little less and she thought of the Japanese woman, a beautiful and problematic thing, if she is Japanese at all, watering her garden when the sky shows rain.



She took the tin-can ferry to Little Moon, where there

was nothing to do but walk along a muddy path to the other end of the island past wind-beaten houses and a church with a missing steeple, a forty-minute march to an abandoned crafts center, quilting and woodcarving maybe and pottery by all means, and then briskly back again. The ferry ran on a schedule and this was reason enough to make the trip now and then.

The plan was to organize time until she could live again.

After the first days back she began to do her breathing exercises. There was bodywork to resume, her regimen of cat stretch and methodical contortion. She worked from the spine outward, moving along the floor on all fours, and she felt her aorta recoil to every blood surge. There were headstands and neckrolls. She stuck out her tongue and panted in tightly timed sequence, internally timed, an exactitude she knew in the bones that were separated by the disks that went rat-a-tat down her back.

But the world was lost inside her.

At night the sky was very near, sprawled in star smoke and gamma cataclysms, but she didn't see it the way she used to, as soul extension, dumb guttural wonder, a thing that lived outside language in the oldest part of her.

She stopped listening to weather reports. She took the weather as it came, chill rain and blowy days and the great hunched boulders in the slant fields, like clan emblems, pulsing with stormlight and story and time. She chopped firewood. She spent hours at the computer screen looking at a live-streaming video feed from the edge of a two-lane road in a city in Finland. It was the middle of the night in Kotka, in Finland, and she watched the screen. It was interesting to her because it was happening now, as she sat here, and because it happened twenty-four hours a day, facelessly, cars entering and leaving Kotka, or just the empty road in the dead times. The dead times were best.

She sat and looked at the screen. It was compelling to her, real enough to withstand the circumstance of nothing going on. It thrived on the circumstance. It was three in the morning in Kotka and she waited for a car to come along—not that she wondered who was in it. It was simply the fact of Kotka. It was the sense of organization, a place contained in an unyielding frame, as it is and as you watch, with a reading of local time in the digital display in a corner of the screen. Kotka was another world but she could see it in its realness, in its hours, minutes and seconds.

She imagined that someone might masturbate to this, the appearance of a car on the road to Kotka in the middle of the night. It made her want to laugh. She chopped firewood. She set aside time every day for the webcam at Kotka. She didn't know the meaning of this feed but took it as an act of floating poetry. It was best in the dead times. It emptied her mind and made her feel the deep silence of other places, the mystery of seeing over the world to a place stripped of everything but a road that approaches and recedes, both realities occurring at once, and the numbers changed in the digital display with an odd and hollow urgency, the seconds advancing toward the minute, the minutes climbing hourward, and she sat and watched, waiting for a car to take fleeting shape on the roadway.

Mariella called, her friend, a writer in New York.

"Are you all right?"

"What am I supposed to say?"

"I don't know. But are you lonely?"

"There ought to be another word for it. Everyone's lonely. This is something else."

"But don't you think. I don't know. It would be easier."

"This is the kind of conversation you ought to have with someone else. I don't know how to have these conversations."

"If you didn't separate yourself. You need to be around familiar people and things. Alone is no good. I know how you felt about him. And how devastating. God. But you don't want to fold up into yourself. I also know you're determined. You're strong-willed in your creepy-crawly way. But you have to direct yourself out of this thing, not into it. Don't fold up."

"Tell me what you're doing."

"Feeding my face. Looking out the window," Mariella said. "Talking to you."

"What are you eating?"

"Carrot sticks."

"This is not feeding your face."

"This is starving my body. I know. They're showing some of his early work at the Film Forum. You didn't know him that long. This could be a plus."

In the morning she heard the noise. It had the same sort of distinctness she'd noted the first time, about three months ago, when she and Rey had gone upstairs to investigate. He said it was a squirrel or raccoon trapped somewhere. She thought it was a calculated stealth. It had a certain measured quality. She didn't think it was an animal noise. It carried an effect that was nearly intimate, like something's here and breathing the same air we breathe and it moves the way we move. The noise had this quality, of a body shedding space, but there was no one there when they looked.

She was in the kitchen when she heard it this time. She carried her tea upstairs. The rooms at the end of the second-story hall. The dim third story, bulbs blown and most of the furniture removed. The short stairway to the cupola. She looked into the stillness, head swiveling, her upper body projected into the structure, which was fairly broad and used as storage space. Her tea was cold by the time she stood on the floor of the cupola. She poked into old clothing layered in cardboard boxes and looked at documents gone brittle in leather folders. There was a stuffed owl and a stack of unframed watercolors, badly warped. She saw a twirling leaf just outside the window. It was a small amber leaf twirling in the air beneath a tree branch that extended over the roof. There was no sign of a larva web from which the leaf might be suspended, or a strand of some bird's nest-building material. Just the leaf in midair, turning.

She found him the next day in a small bedroom off the large empty room at the far end of the hall on the third floor. He was smallish and fine-bodied and at first she thought he was a kid, sandy-haired and roused from deep sleep, or medicated maybe.

He sat on the edge of the bed in his underwear. In the first seconds she thought he was inevitable. She felt her way back in time to the earlier indications that there was someone in the house and she arrived at this instant, unerringly, with her perceptions all sorted and endorsed.

# CHAPTER 3

She looked at him.

"Tell me. You've been here how long?"

He didn't raise his head. There was something so strange about him that she heard her words hang in the room, predictable and trite. She felt no fear. He had a foundling quality—lost and found—and she was, she guessed, the finder.

"You have been here," she said, speaking clearly, pausing between words.

He looked at her and seemed older now, the scant act of head-raising, a simple tilt of chin and eyes that was minutely crucial to his transformation—older and faintly moist, a sheen across his forehead and cheeks.

He said something.

She said, "What?"

His underwear consisted of white trunks and a T-shirt that was too big and she studied him up and down, openly, everywhere.

"It is not able," he said.

"But why are you here? And have you been here for long?"

He dropped his head and appeared to think about these matters as if working out the details of a complicated problem.

They stood outside the house near the top of the sloped field and watched a lobsterboat pumping through the whitecaps. She'd fed him leftover soup and some bread, some toast. You had to flip the thing twice to get the bread to toast properly.

"What do you see?" she said, gesturing toward the boat and the advancing cloudline.

"The trees are some of them," he said.

"Bending. Swaying in the wind. Those are birches. The white ones. Those are called paper birches."

"The white ones."

"The white ones. But beyond the trees."

"Beyond the trees."

"Out there," she said.

He looked a while.

"It rained very much."

"It will rain. It is going to rain," she said.

He wore a windbreaker and a pair of workpants and seemed unhappy out here. She tried not to press him for information. She found the distance interesting, the halting quality of his speech and actions, the self-taught quality, his seeming unconcern about what would happen to him now. Not apathy or indifference, she thought, but his limited ability to consider the implications. She wasn't sure what it meant to him, being found in someone else's house.

The wind came harder now and they turned away from it. She amused herself by thinking he'd come from cyberspace, a man who'd emerged from her computer screen in the dead of night. He was from Kotka, in Finland.

She said, "It did not rain. It *will* rain."

He moved uneasily in space, indoors or out, as if the air had bends and warps. She watched him sidle into the house, walking with a slight shuffle. He feared levitation maybe. She could not stop watching him.

It was always as if. He did this or that as if. She needed a reference elsewhere to get him placed.

They sat in the grim panelled room under prints of sailing ships. The phone was ringing. He looked at the charred logs collapsed in the fireplace, last night's fire, and she watched him. The books on the low shelves were mostly summer reading you find in rented houses, books suited to the role, with faded jacket illustrations of other houses in other summers, or almanacs, or atlases, a sun stripe edging the tops of the taller books.

His chin was sunken back, severely receded, giving his face an unfinished look, and his hair was wiry and snagged, with jutting clumps.

She had to concentrate to note these features. She looked at him and had to look again. There was something elusive in his aspect, moment to moment, a thinness of physical address.

She whispered, "Talk to me."

He sat with his legs awkwardly crossed, one trouser leg riding up his calf, and she could see that he'd knotted a length of string around the top of his sock to keep it from sagging. It made her think of someone.

"Talk to me. I am talking," he said.

She thought she understood what he meant by this. There was a certain futility in his tone, an endlessness of effort, suggesting things he could not easily make clear to her no matter how much he said. Even his gestures seemed marked by struggle. She knew she would have to call hospitals and clinics, psychiatric facilities, to ask about a missing patient.

The rain hit the windows in taps and spatters, small and countable, and then it was everywhere, banging the roof of the sunporch and filling the downspouts, and they sat and listened to it.

She said, "What's your name?"

He looked at her.

She said, "I came here to be by myself. This is important to me. I am willing to wait. I will give you a chance to tell me who you are. But I don't want someone in my house. I will give you a chance," she said. "But I will not wait indefinitely."

She didn't want it to sound like a formal warning but it probably did. She would have to call the nearest mission for the homeless, which wouldn't be near at all, and maybe the church in town or the church with the missing steeple on Little Moon and she would have to call the police, finally, if nothing else worked.

"I am here because of Rey, who was my husband, who is dead. I don't know why I'm telling you this because it is surely unnecessary. But I need to live here alone for a time. Just tell me if you understand."

He moved his hand in a manner that seemed to mean she didn't have to say anything further. Of course he understood. But maybe not.

The storm rolled in and they sat and listened. The rain was so total they had to listen to it. She could call the real estate agent and make a complaint about a person on the premises. That was another thing she could do.

It was only midmorning but she had the feeling he'd been here a week. They sat and looked at last night's fire.

Then she realized who it was, the man he made her think of.

It was a science teacher in high school, semi-bumbling, who looked pale-haired in uncertain light and bald on brighter days and who scotch-taped a split seam in his loafers once and spoke in unmeasured hesitations that made the students feel embarrassed on his behalf, the few sensitive ones, or openly restless, the restless, which was everybody else.

She named the visitor in his honor. Mr. Tuttle. She thought it would make him easier to see.

She whispered, "Tell me something."

He uncrossed his legs and sat with a hand on each knee, a dummy in a red club chair, his head turned toward her.

"I know how much." He said, "I know how much this house. Alone by the sea."

He looked not pleased exactly but otherwise satisfied, technically satisfied to have managed the last cluster of words. And it was in fact, coming from Mr. Tuttle, a formulation she heard in its echoing depths. Four words only. But he'd placed her in a set of counter-surroundings, of simultaneous insides and outsides. The house, the sea-planet outside it, and how the word *alone* referred to her and to the house and how the word *sea* reinforced the idea of solitude but suggested a vigorous release as well, a means of escape from the book-walled limits of the self.

She knew it was foolish to examine so closely. She was making things up. But this was the effect he had, shadow-inching through a sentence, showing a word in its facets and aspects, words like moons in particular phases.

She said, "I like the house. Yes, I want to be here. But it's only a rental. I am renting. I will be out of here in six or seven weeks. Less maybe. It's a house we rented. Five or six weeks. Less," she said.

She wasn't watching him now. She was looking at the backs of her hands, fingers stretched, looking and thinking, recalling moments with Rey, not moments exactly but times, or moments flowing into composite time, an erotic of see and touch, and she curled one hand over and into the other, missing him in her body and feeling sexually and abysmally alone and staring at the points where her knuckles shone bloodless from the pressure of her grip.

He said, "But you did not leave."

She looked at him.

"I will leave. In a few weeks. When it's time," she said. "When the lease is up. Or earlier. I will leave."

"But you do not," he said.

This shift from past tense to present had the sound of something overcome, an obstacle or restriction. He had to extend himself to get it out. And she heard something in his voice. She didn't know what it was but it made her get up and go to the window.

She stood there looking at the rain. She thought he might belong in one of the trailer homes scattered at the edge of the woods outside town, near but wholly remote, with cars on blocks and a wacko dog convoluted in the dirt and leaves, trying to scratch an itch somewhere, and he is the grown son who has always been this way, inaccessible, ever dependent, living matter-of-fact in an oblong box with his drained and aging parents, who never use each other's name, and he wanders off for days sometimes and goes wherever he goes, muttering and unharmed, into the bubble world.

Maybe not, she thought. That's not what she'd heard in his voice. There was something at the edge, unconnected to income levels or verb tenses or what his parents watch on TV.

She turned from the window and got him to talk a little. He seemed agreeable to the idea of talking. He talked about objects in the room, stumblingly, and she wondered what he saw, or failed to see, or saw so differently she could never begin to conjure its outlines.

He talked. After a while she began to understand what she was hearing. It took many levels of perception. It took whole social histories of how people listen to what other people say. There was a peculiarity in his voice, a trait developing even as he spoke, that she was able to follow to its source.

She watched him. He was the same hapless man she'd come upon earlier, without a visible sense of the effect he was having.

It wasn't outright impersonation but she heard elements of her voice, the clipped delivery, the slight buzz deep in the throat, her pitch, her sound, and how difficult at first, unearthly almost, to detect her own voice coming from someone else, from him, and then how deeply disturbing.

She wasn't sure it was her voice. Then she was. By this time he wasn't talking about chairs, lamps or patterns in the carpet. He seemed to be assuming her part in a conversation with someone.

She tried to understand what she was hearing.

He gestured as he spoke, moving his hand to the words, and she began to realize she'd said these things to Rey, here in the house, or things similar. They were routine remarks about a call she'd had from friends who wanted to visit. She remembered, she recalled dimly that she'd been standing at the foot of the stairs and that he'd been on the second floor, Rey had, walking up and down the hall, doing scriptwork.

She stood by the window now. The voice began to waver and fade but his hand remained in motion, marking the feeble beat.

She grabbed a coat from the rack and went out in the rain. She draped the coat over her bent arm, which she held above her, and walked across the grass to the dirt driveway, where the car was parked. The door was unlocked and she got in and sat there because why would you lock the door in a place so isolated. Rain washed down the windshield in overlapping tides. She sat there in a brief fit of shivering and it was hard to stop hearing the sound of that voice. One of the rear windows was lowered an inch and the smell of wet meadow, the fragrance of country rain, the effects of sea and breeze and memory all mixed in the air but she kept hearing the voice and seeing the hand gesture, unmistakably Rey's, two fingers joined and wagging.

She didn't know how long she was there. Maybe a long time. The rain beat hard on the roof and hood. How much time is a long time? Could be this, could be that. Finally she pushed open the door and walked back to the house, holding the coat aloft.

# CHAPTER 4

There were five birds on the feeder and they all faced outward, away from the food and identically still. She watched them. They weren't looking or listening so much as feeling something, intent and sensing.

All these words are wrong, she thought.

This was the feeder that hung outside the sunporch and she stood in the mostly white room, by the broad window, waiting for Mr. Tuttle.

She'd been putting up feeders since her return. This was the basic range of her worldly surround, the breadth of nature that bordered the house. But it feels like she's feeding the birds of Earth, a different seed for each receptacle, sometimes two seeds layered light and dark in a single feeder, and they come and peck, or don't, and the feeders are different as well, cages, ringed cylinders, hanging saucers, mounted trays, and maybe it's a hawk, she doesn't know, that keeps the birds away sometimes, or a jay that mimics a hawk, or they read a message in some event outside the visible spectrum.

When he walked in he didn't look at her but went straight to the glass-top table with the curlicued legs.

Rey's tape recorder lay blinking in the middle of the table.

She sat and began to speak, describing his appearance. Face and hair and so forth. Wakeful or not. Fairly neat or mostly unkempt. What else? Good, bad or indifferent night.

Not that she knew what his nights were like. One night only. She hadn't been able to sleep and had stood for a while at his door past midnight, listening to the raspy nasal intake and finding herself moved in an unusual way. In sleep he was no more unknowable than anyone else. Look. The shrouded body feebly beating. This is what you feel, looking at the hushed and vulnerable body, almost anyone's, or you lie next to your husband after you've made love and breathe the heat of his merciless dreams and wonder who he is, tenderly ponder the truth you'll never know, because this is the secret that sleep protects in its neural depths, in its stages, layers and folds.

This morning she talked about his name, or tried to. They did it together, start and stop. But the more they talked—they talked a while and changed the subject and he turned off the recorder and she turned it back on and maybe he'd had one, yes, a name, but he'd forgotten it or lost it and could not get it back.



She said, "I am Lauren."

She said this a number of times, pointing at herself, because she thought it would be helpful to both of them if he called her by her name.

She said, "If you had a name. Just suppose now. Is there anyone who would know what it is? Where is your mother? When I say mother, the woman who gives birth to a child, the parent, the female parent, does this word? Tell me. What?"

He knew what a chair is called and a window and a wall but not the tape recorder, although he knew how to turn it off, and not, it seemed, who his mother was or where she might be found.

"If there is another language you speak," she told him, "say some words."

"Say some words."

"Say some words. Doesn't matter if I can't understand."

"Say some words to say some words."

"All right. Be a Zen master, you little creep. How do you know what I said to my husband? Where were you? Were you here, somewhere, listening? My voice. It sounded word for word. Tell me about this."

When there was a pause in the conversation, the recorder stopped hissing. She watched him. She tried to press him on the matter but got nowhere and changed the subject again.

"What did you mean earlier yesterday when you said, when you seemed to say what? I don't recall the words exactly. It was yesterday. The day before today. You said I'd still be here, I think, when the lease. Do you remember this? When I'm supposed to leave. You said I do not."

"I said this what I said."

"You said this. That you somehow."

"Somehow. What is somehow?"

"Shut up. That you somehow but never mind. When the lease ends. Or something else completely."

He turned off the recorder. She turned it on, he turned it off. Just curious, she thought, or aimlessly playing. But she felt like hitting him. No, she didn't. She didn't know what she felt. It was time to call the hospitals and other institutions. That's what she felt. It was way past the time and she was making a mistake not to inquire, not to take him to someone in a position of authority, a doctor or administrator, the nun who runs an assisted-living shelter, gracious and able, but she knew she would not do it.

She spent an hour in a makeshift office on the second floor, transcribing selected remarks from the tape she'd made with him.

She heard herself say, "I am Lauren," like a character in black spandex in a science-fiction film.

It occurred to her finally. She began to understand that he'd heard her voice on the tape recorder. At some point before she'd inserted a blank tape, he'd hit the play button and heard her talking to Rey, who was up on the second floor with the tape machine in his hand, communicating script ideas.

That's how he reproduced her voice.

What about the hand gesture? She rejected the hand gesture. The gesture was coincidental, circumstantial, partly her own fabrication.

She felt better now.

Over the days she worked her body hard. There were always states to reach that surpassed previous extremes. She could take a thing to an unendurable extreme as measured by breath or strength or length of time or force of will and then resolve to extend the limit.

I think you are making your own little totalitarian society, Rey told her once, where you are the dictator, absolutely, and also the oppressed people, he said, perhaps admiringly, one artist to another.

Her bodywork made everything transparent. She saw and thought clearly, which might only mean there was little that needed seeing and not a lot to think about. But maybe it went deeper, the poses she assumed and held for prolonged periods, the gyrate exaggerations, the snake shapes and flower bends, the prayerful spans of systematic breathing, life lived irreducibly as sheer respiration. First breathe, then pant, then gasp. It made her go taut and saucer-eyed, arteries flaring in her neck, these hours of breathing so urgent and absurd that she came out the other end in a kind of pristine light, feeling what it means to be alive.

She began to work naked in a cold room. She did her crossovers on the bare floor, and her pelvic stretches, which were mockingly erotic and erotic both, and her slow-motion repetitions of everyday gestures, checking the time on your wrist or turning to hail a cab, actions quoted by rote in another conceptual frame, many times over and now slower and over, with your mouth open in astonishment and your eyes shut tight against the intensity of passing awareness.

Isabel called, Rey's first wife.

"At the funeral we barely talked. So you avoided me a little, which I understand it, believe me, and can sympathize. I also accept what he did because I know him forever. But for you it's different. I feel bad we didn't talk. I could see it coming for years. This is a thing that was going to happen. We all knew this about him. For years he was going to do this thing. It was a thing he carried with him. It was his way out. He wasn't a man in despair. This thing was a plan in his mind. It was his trick that he knew he could do when he needed it. He even made me see him in the chair."

"But don't you understand?"

"Please. Who understands but me? He was an impossible man. From Paris already he was very difficult. Nearly eleven years we were married. I went through things with him I could not begin to tell you. Don't think I am not sparing you. I am sparing you everything. This man, it was not a question of chemicals in his brain. It was him who he was. Frankly you didn't have time to find out. Because I will tell you something. We were two people with one life and it was his life. I stayed with him until it ruined my health, which I am still paying the price. I had to leave in the middle of the night. Because why do you think? He threatened he would kill me. And in this room where I'm standing I look at the empty space where the chair used to be. For one whole day it was here until they removed it out of my sight and took it to the medical examiner, with his blood and what else, I won't even describe, okay, for evidence. So I buy another chair. No problem. In the meantime there is the empty space. Of course he wanted to spare you the actual moment. So he comes to New York and sits in my chair."

"It was your chair. Was it your gun? Whose gun did he use?"

"Are you crazy my gun? This is another thing you didn't know. He always owned a gun. Wherever he lived he had a gun. This gun or that gun. I didn't keep count."

"No. Don't you understand? I don't want to hear this."

"But I want to say it. I insist to say it. This man hated who he was. Because how long do I know this man and how long do you know him? I never left. Did I ever leave? Were we ever really separated? I knew him in my sleep. And I know exactly how his mind was working. He said to himself two things. This is a woman I know forever. And maybe she will not mind the mess."

She went looking for Mr. Tuttle. She had no idea where he went or what he did when he was out of her sight. He made more sense to her sleeping than he did across the table, eyes slightly bulging, or in her imagination for that matter. It was hard for her to think him into being, even momentarily, in the shallowest sort of conjecture, a figure by a window in the dusty light.

She stood in the front hall and called, "Where are you?"

That night they sat in the panelled room and she read to him from a book about the human body. There were photographs of blood cells magnified many thousands of times and there was a section of text on the biology of childbirth and this is what she was reading to him, slowly, inserting comments of her own, and asking questions, and drinking tea, and about forty minutes into the session, reading a passage about the embryo, half an inch long, afloat in body fluid, she realized he was talking to her.

But it was Rey's voice she was hearing. The representation was close, the accent and dragged vowels, the intimate differences, the articulations produced in one vocal apparatus and not another, things she'd known in

Rey's voice, and only Rey's, and she kept her head in the book, unable to look at him.

She tried to concentrate on strict listening. She told herself to listen. Her hand was still in the air, measuring the embryo for him, thumb and index finger setting the length.

She followed what he said, word for word, but had to search for the context. The speech rambled and spun. He was talking about cigarette brands, Players and Gitanes, I'd walk a mile for a Camel, and then she heard Rey's, the bell-clap report of Rey's laughter, clear and spaced, and this did not come from a tape recorder.

He was talking to her, not to a screenwriter in Rome or Los Angeles. It was Rey in his role of charming fatalist, reciting the history of his addiction to nicotine, and she heard her name along the way, the first time Mr. Tuttle had used it.

This was not some communication with the dead. It was Rey alive in the course of a talk he'd had with her, in this room, not long after they'd come here. She was sure of this, recalling how they'd gone upstairs and dropped into a night of tossing sensation, drifts of sex, confession and pale sleep, and it was confession as belief in each other, not unburdenings of guilt but avowals of belief, mostly his and stricken by need, and then drowsy sex again, two people passing through each other, easy and airy as sea spray, and how he'd told her that she was helping him recover his soul.

All this a white shine somewhere, an iceblink of memory, and then the words themselves, Rey's words, being spoken by the man in the chair nearby.

"I regain possession of myself through you. I think like myself now, not like the man I became. I eat and sleep like myself, bad, which is bad, but it's like myself when I was myself and not the other man."

She looked at him, a cartoon head and body, chinless, stick-figured, but he knew how to make her husband live in the air that rushed from his lungs into his vocal folds—air to sounds, sounds to words, words the man, shaped faithfully on his lips and tongue.

She whispered, "What are you doing?"

"I am doing. This yes that. Say some words."

"Did you ever? Look at me. Did you ever talk to Rey? The way we are talking now."

"We are talking now."

"Yes. Are you saying yes? Say yes. When did you know him?"

"I know him where he was."

"Then and now. Is that what you're saying? Did you stand outside the room and hear us talking? When I say Rey, do you know who I mean? Talking in a room. He and I."

He let his body shift, briefly, side to side, a mechanical wag, a tick and a tock, like the first toy ever built with moving parts.



She didn't know how to think about this. There was

something raw in the moment, open-wounded. It bared her to things that were outside her experience but desperately central, somehow, at the same time.

Somehow. What is somehow?

She asked him questions and he talked in his own voice, which was reedy and thin and trapped in tenses and inflections, in singsong conjugations, and she became aware that she was describing what he said to some third person in her mind, maybe her friend Mariella, objective, dependable, able to advise, known to be frank, even as she listened possessively to every word he spoke.

She began to carry the tape recorder everywhere she went. It was small and light and slipped into her breast pocket. She wore flannel shirts with flap pockets. She wore insulated boots and walked for hours along the edge of saltgrass marshes and down the middle of lost roads and she listened to Mr. Tuttle.

She looked at her face in the bathroom mirror and tried to understand why it looked different from the same face downstairs, in the full-length mirror in the front hall, although it shouldn't be hard to understand at all, she thought, because faces look different all the time and everywhere, based on a hundred daily variables, but then again, she thought, why do I look different?

• • •

She didn't take him into town because someone might know him there and because he never left the house by choice, to her knowledge, and she didn't want to force him into an experience that might frighten him, but mostly she wanted to keep him from being seen by others.

But then she took him with her to the sprawling malls, inland, in the thickness of car smog and nudging traffic, and she did it the way you do something even stranger than all the things you judged too strange to do, on impulse, to ease a need for rash gestures and faintly and vainly perhaps to see things through his eyes, the world in geometric form, patterned and stacked, and the long aisles of products and the shoppers in soft-shoe trance and whatever else might warrant his regard that you have forgotten how to see.

But when they got there she left him strapped in his seatbelt and locked in the car while she went to the electronics store and supermarket and shoe outlet. She bought him a pair of shoes and some socks. She bought blank tapes for the voice recorder, unavailable in town, and came back to the car with bags of groceries in a gleaming cart and found him sitting in piss and shit.

Maybe this man experiences another kind of reality where he is here and there, before and after, and he moves from one to the other shatteringly, in a state of collapse, minus an identity, a language, a way to enjoy the savor of the honey-coated toast she watches him eat.

She thought maybe he lived in a kind of time that had no narrative quality. What else did she think? She sat in the nearly bare office on the second floor and didn't know what else she thought.

They spoke every morning at the glass-top table on the sunporch and she recorded what they said. The room was unheated but they sat comfortably in the current run of sunny days over mugs of mint tea.

He sat hunched, speaking toward the device, sometimes into it, seemingly to it, with it, just he and it, and when he stopped cold, between constructions, his mouth continued to vibrate slightly, a shadow movement that resembled an old person's tremor of reflex or agitation.

"Did you know Rey? Do you know who I mean when I say Rey?"

"It is not able."

"Try to answer. Please. You see how important it is to me. Talk like him. Say some words."

There's a code in the simplest conversation that tells the speakers what's going on outside the bare acoustics. This was missing when they talked. There was a missing beat. It was hard for her to find the tempo. All they had were unadjusted words. She lost touch with him, lost interest sometimes, couldn't locate rhythmic intervals or time cues or even the mutters and hums, the audible pauses that pace a remark. He didn't register facial responses to things she said and this threw her off. There were no grades of emphasis here and flatness there. She began to understand that their talks had no time sense and that all the references at the unspoken level, the things a man speaking Dutch might share with a man speaking Chinese—all this was missing here.

"Push the thing."

"Push the button. No, do not push the button. That's the stop button. Did you hear us in the room? He and I. Talking."

She wanted to touch him. She'd never touched him, she didn't think, or did passingly, maybe, once, strapping him into his seat in the car, when he was wearing a sweater or jacket.

"You know him where he was. You know him from before. You heard him speak to me. Did we see you? Were you hidden somewhere so we could not see you? Understand hidden? You know his voice. Make me hear it."

She knew, she told herself she was not an unstrung woman who encounters a person responsive to psychic forces, able to put her in touch with her late husband.

This was something else.

She watched him. His hair looked chalky today. He seemed barely here, four feet away from her. He didn't know how to measure himself to what we call the Now. What is that anyway? It's possible there's no such thing for those who do not take it as a matter of faith. Maybe it was a physicist she needed to talk to, someone, she wasn't sure, who might tell her what the parameters were. She hated that word. She used it but didn't know what it meant and used it anyway. The birds were going crazy on the feeder.

She called Mariella and got the machine. A synthesized voice said, *Please / leave / a mess/age / af/ter / the / tone.* The words were not spoken but generated and they were separated by brief but deep dimensions. She hung up and called back, just to hear the voice again. How strange the discontinuity. It seemed a quantum hop, one word to the next. She hung up and called back. One voice for each word. Seven different voices. Not seven different voices but one male voice in seven time cycles. But not male exactly either. And not words so much as syllables but not that either. She hung up and called back.

She walked down the long hall and up the stairs to the third floor and past the empty rooms to the bathroom near the far end. He was sitting in the tub when she opened the door. He did not move his head or in any way acknowledge. She stood there looking. He had soap in one hand and a washcloth in the other. He remained in this position, hands poised, and she watched him. He did not move. He did not look at her or acknowledge by other means. His hands were barely out of the water, the sliver of soap, the washcloth bunched. Soap is called a sliver in this figuration.

She whispered, "Look at me."

When he did this, unbashfully, she got on her knees at the side of the tub and took the washcloth out of his hand. She moved it side to side over his shoulders and down his back. She washed in the hollow under the arm. This is the armpit, one and two. She took the soap out of his other hand and rubbed it on the cloth and washed his chest and arms, wordlessly naming his parts for him. She set the cloth down gently on the water, where it plumed inward and sank, and she swabbed his belly under the water with the soap, a drone of motion, her hand slowly circling his navel. Then she leaned across him to place the soap in the soap dish, the sliver of soap, watching him all the time, and she put her hand in the water and eased along the penis, here it is, and cupped and rubbed the testicles, naming and numbering his parts, one and two, and a small moist glow showed above his lips.

His hand came out of the water holding the cloth. She took it from him and held it spread across her face and pressed into the pores and she rubbed it over her mouth and gave it back to him. She touched his face, which was lightly fuzzed, and does he shave and who taught him, and ran her finger softly across his mouth, tracing the shape of his lips. She traced his nose and brows and the rim of his ear and the swirled inner surface. This followed by that. This leading to that. He was not skittish under her touch, or only routinely so, and she thought that nothing could seem unusual to him, or startling, or stirring, measured against the fact, the blur, whatever it was—the breathless shock of his being here.

She felt something wispy at the edge of her mouth, half in half out, that could only be a hair. She plucked at it and brushed with her thumb, a strand of hair from the washcloth, and she couldn't feel it on her face anymore and she looked at him and looked at her hand and maybe it was just an itch.

Then she went back down the hall and of course it did not feel to her that she'd been washing a child but then it wasn't quite a man either but then, again, this was who he was, outside the easy sway of either/or, and she was still finding things to examine, and wondering aloud about his use of a washcloth, which seemed a high refinement, and defending herself for her actions, and analyzing her own response to the motion of her hand over his body as she walked for miles through the blueberry barrens, in blowing mist, jacket fastened and tape reels turning.

"How could you be living here without my knowing?"

"But you know. I am living."

He half hit himself on the cheek, a little joke perhaps.

"But before. I hear a noise and you are in a room

upstairs. For how long were you here? Talk into the thing."

"Talk into the thing," he said in a voice that may have been an unintended imitation of hers.

She was in town, driving down a hilly street of frame houses, and saw a man sitting on his porch, ahead of her, through trees and shrubs, arms spread, a broad-faced blondish man, lounging. She felt in that small point in time, a flyspeck quarter second or so, that she saw him complete. His life flew open to her passing glance. A lazy and manipulative man, in real estate, in fairview condos by a mosquito lake. She knew him. She saw into him. He was there, divorced and drink-haunted, emotionally distant from his kids, his sons, two sons, in school blazers, in the barest blink.

A voice recited the news on the radio.

When the car moved past the house, in the pull of the full second, she understood that she was not looking at a seated man but at a paint can placed on a board that was balanced between two chairs. The white and yellow can was his face, the board was his arms and the mind and heart of the man were in the air somewhere, already lost in the voice of the news reader on the radio.

She called Mariella's number and got the machine. She listened to the recording and hung up and then called again and hung up. She called several times over the next day and a half and listened to the recorded voice and did not leave a message. When she called again and Mariella answered, she put down the phone, softly, and stood completely still.

She said, "Talk like him. I want you to do this for me. I know you are able to do it. Do it for me. Talk like him. Say something he said that you remember. Or say whatever comes into your head. That is better. Say whatever comes into your head, just so it is him. I will not ask you how you are able to do it. I only want to listen. Talk like him. Do like him. Speak in his voice. Do Rey. Make me hear him. I am asking you nice. Be my friend. A trusted person, this is a friend. Do this for me."

They came flying in straight-up to the rungs, fighting for space at the feeding ports, pecking at others, wings humming and breasts burnt white in the sun, feed spilling from their beaks. They flew off and came back, semi-hovering, nine, ten, eleven birds, others fixed to the window screen, some in trees nearby, not singing exactly but what's the word, twitter or peep or squeak, and they attacked each other on the rungs or scrambling in midair, the color-changing birds, the name-saying birds, the birds that feed upside down.

At night she stood outside his room and watched him sleep. She stayed for an hour and then went on-line to look at the cars start to appear on the two-lane highway that entered and left Kotka, in Finland, watching until she was able to sleep herself, finally, with the arrival of nordic light.

## CHAPTER 5

It was another slow morning, foggy and still, and the phone was ringing. She stood nude in the workout room, bent left, eyes shut, checking the time on her wrist.

Or sat cross-legged, back straight, breathing dementedly. She blew through her nostrils and made echoey sounds in her throat, visualizing her body lifting and spinning, a rotation with every breath.

Or went about on all fours, knees hip-distance apart, rump up, feeling the cat-length in her pose, doing the shoulder roll.

She stood and swung slowly about, eternally checking the time, half her body wheeling with the arc of the left arm, the watch arm, or the body levered by the arm and the head cranking incrementally like the second hand on the missing watch, mouth open and eyes ever tight.

She heard a plane cross the sky and then the light blinked off and on, the sunlight, the sunray, an event she assembled through closed lids, and she knew the fog had finally lifted.

When it was too damp and cold on the sunporch, they talked in the panelled room and she took notes and recorded. He barely spoke some mornings but was willing on others and they sat near the fire she'd built and the house was dead around them.

"Being here has come to me. I am with the moment, I will leave the moment. Chair, table, wall, hall, all for the moment, in the moment. It has come to me. Here and near. From the moment I am gone, am left, am leaving. I will leave the moment from the moment."

She didn't know what to call this. She called it singing. He kept it going a while, ongoing, oncoming, and it was song, it was chant. She leaned into him. This was a level that demonstrated he was not closed to inspiration. She felt an easing in her body that drew her down out of laborious thought and into something nearly uncontrollable. She leaned into his voice, laughing. She wanted to chant with him, to fall in and out of time, or words, or things, whatever he was doing, but she only laughed instead.

"Coming and going I am leaving. I will go and come. Leaving has come to me. We all, shall all, will all be left. Because I am here and where. And I will go or not or never. And I have seen what I will see. If I am where I will be. Because nothing comes between me."

She was laughing but he was not. It came out of him nonstop and it wasn't schizophrenic speech or the whoop of rippling bodies shocked by God. He sat pale and still. She watched him. It was pure chant, transparent, or was he saying something to her? She felt an elation that made it hard for her to listen carefully. Was he telling her what it is like to be him, to live in his body and mind? She tried to hear this but could not. The words ran on, sensuous and empty, and she wanted him to laugh with her, to follow her out of herself. This is the point, yes, this is the stir of true amazement. And some terror at the edge, or fear of believing, some displacement of self, but this is the point, this is the wedge into ecstasy, the old deep meaning of the word, your eyes rolling upward in your skull.

"What is the moment? You said the moment. Tell me what this means to you. Show me the moment."

He said, "Talk into the thing."

"What do you know? Who is Rey? Do you talk to him? Did you ever talk to him? Do you know who I am talking about when I say Rey? I am Lauren. Who is Rey? A man. So tall. Look. So tall. This tall. And a mustache. A man with hair on his upper lip. Look at me, geek. How tall? This tall. A man with brushy hair on his upper lip. But then he shaved his mustache."

He shaved his mustache. She'd forgotten this until now.

• • •

She saw something out of the corner of her eye. She turned her head and nothing was there. The phone was ringing. She decided to find an optometrist because she thought she'd seen something a number of times, or once or twice, out of the corner of her right eye, or an ophthalmologist, but knew she wouldn't bother. The phone was ringing. She picked it up and waited for someone to speak.

It was time to sand her body. She used a pumice stone on the bottoms of her feet, working circular swipes, balls, heels, and then resoaped the foot and twisted it up into her hand again. She liked to hold a foot in a hand. She patiently razed the lone callus, stretching the task over days, lost in it, her body coiled in a wholeness of intent, the kind of solemn self-absorption that marks a line from childhood.

She had emery boards and files, many kinds of scissors, clippers and creams that activated the verbs of abridgment and excision. She studied her fingers and toes. There was a way in which she isolated a digit for sharp regard, using a magnifier and a square of dark cardboard, and there were hangnails flying and shreds and grains of dead skin and fragments of nail, scintillas, springing in the air.

It was good to be doing this again.



• • •

Maybe this man is defenseless against the truth of the world.

What truth? She thought, What truth?

Time is supposed to pass, she thought. But maybe he is living in another state. It is a kind of time that is simply and overwhelmingly there, laid out, unoccurring, and he lacks the inborn ability to reconceive this condition.

What ability?

There is nothing he can do to imagine time existing in reassuring sequence, passing, flowing, happening—the world happens, it has to, we feel it—with names and dates and distinctions.

His future is unnamed. It is simultaneous, somehow, with the present. Neither happens before or after the other and they are equally accessible, perhaps, if only in his mind.

The laws of nature permit things that in fact, in practice, she thought, never happen.

But could.

But could not.

But could. If only in his mind, she thought.

She ate dull light dinners, quickly, getting it over with. Sometimes he didn't appear and sometimes he appeared but didn't eat and once he was missing for six or seven hours and she went through the house and then down the driveway in the dark, shining a flashlight in the trees and calmly saying, "Where are you?"

She waited inside with a book in her hands, a prop, sitting and thinking, not thinking, any woman who knows the worst.

He came into the room then, edgingly, in his self-winding way, as if, as if. She watched him try to adapt his frame to a wing chair and allowed herself a certain measure of relief, a kind of body lightness that disengaged her dreamily from the stolid woman with the book.

She thought of a man showing up unexpectedly. Not the man who was here now. Another man. It was nothing, it was something that came into her mind while she ate her breakfast, a man appearing suddenly, as in a movie, and he is shot from below. Not shot but photographed. Not shot-shot but captured on motion-picture film, from below, so that he looms. It comes as a shock, the way it's done, a man at the door, lighted in such and such a way, menacingly, for effect, or encountered in the driveway when she gets out of her car, a large man, looming suddenly above her. It is the shock of the outside world, the blow, the stun of intrusion, and the moment is rendered in a way that's deeply threatening to two people who have been living reclusively, in self-involved circumstances. It turns out that he is the owner of the house, a large man, yes, for effect, old but fit, or not so old, and it turns out further that he is here to talk about Mr. Tuttle.



She saw herself in the scene, in the driveway, listening

to the man. It was just a passing thing, a story she told herself, or screened, forgettably. The man explains to her that Mr. Tuttle, by whatever name, is a family member of the second cousin type, or he is the son, this is better, of a beloved sister, and he has spent much of his life in this house, with an undiagnosed condition, or brain-damaged, better, and being cared for part-time by a nurse hired by the man, the owner, who is a little tweedy, a little shabby but mostly sad, sort of family sad, and when the owner and his wife Alma resolved to live elsewhere, with the children grown and starting families of their own, they decided to rent this old lopsided pile, their memoried hearth and home, and eventually probably sell, and they put Mr. Tuttle, whose real name does not get used, into a facility for people suffering from one sort of condition or another, a hundred miles from here, states of being that are beyond the most reckless surmise, and it never occurred to the family, when they heard he was missing from the facility, that he might be capable of finding his way back to the house, until now. It has occurred to them now, and so here he is, the owner, inquiring.

She refrains, in her imagining, as does the owner, from using the lost dog analogy as it pertains to Mr. Tuttle, out of whatever scruple and so on, and that was how the thing ended, more or less, over breakfast, with the owner and the tenant in the driveway, looking vaguely at the house.

The name Alma came out of nowhere. It seemed completely believable. Everything seemed believable, even the lost dog return, and the thing about the scene is that it never reached the point of does she turn him in, does she give him up, but just ended, abruptly, like this.

She walked on the grounds, feeling what was here, all sky and light, the sound of hammering somewhere in one of the hutments off the dirt road, nearly half a mile off, tactful on the wind, and how the clarity of things can deepen your step, give you something to catch at and grip, and then the hammer stopped. She walked and thought. It was one of the birdless mornings. A stillness hung about the feeders, such emptiness, arresting in its depth.

Inside she noticed first thing that he was wearing the shoes she'd bought him, snug, laced, with cushioned soles, and she was pleased about this.

They sat in the panelled room with the tape device on a coffee table between them.

Who had taught him to tie his shoes?

He was staring at her. He seemed to be staring but probably wasn't. She didn't think his eye was able to search out and shape things. Not like normal anyway. The eye is supposed to shape and process and paint. It tells us a story we want to believe.

"Then when it comes to me."

"What?"

"A thing of the most. Days yes years."

"Do you know what that means? A day. A year. Or did you hear me use these words?"

"Say some words."

"Say some words."

"In when it comes."

"In when it comes. What?" she said.

"Leave into leaving."

"Who is leaving?"

"This is when you, yes, you said."

"What did I say?"

She realized she'd never called him by his name. She spoke his name only when she was alone, talking into the tape recorder. Because, of course, admit it—the name is cute and condescending.

He said, "Don't touch it," in a voice that wasn't quite his. "I'll clean it up later."

He fell into a silence after this. Yes, fell. Showing a downcast glance, a lowering of spirits if she read it right. She recited a nursery rhyme, in French. She tried to get him to repeat a line and he made an effort, touching and hopeless, and she found herself describing the scene, mentally, to someone who may have been Mariella, or not, as if he were a piece of found art and they needed, between them, to settle the question of his usability.

Afternoons, ever so fast, last light drained into the hills across the bay, into everything around her, trees and earth and the pressed leaves beneath her feet, umbered rust and gold, and once a skein of geese passed silently over her shoulder, flying down the world into their secret night.

She began to understand that she could not miss Rey, could not consider his absence, the loss of Rey, without thinking along the margins of Mr. Tuttle.

When she picked up the ringing phone, she waited for the caller to speak first and felt a small cruel satisfaction in the lull of puzzled molecules.

She took him outside on a clear night and traced a constellation with her finger. It was a while since she'd looked at the night sky and their breath showed smoky in the chill air. She drew him frontally near and put his hands in her jacket pockets and blew words in his face that she made him repeat.

He said, "The word for moonlight is moonlight."

This made her happy. It was logically complex and oddly moving and circularly beautiful and true—or maybe not so circular but straight as straight can be.

She had to find a name that she could call him to his face.

She found it interesting to think that he lived in overlapping realities.

Many things are interesting, fool, but nowhere near true.

She reminded herself she needed batteries for the tape recorder.

She liked to think. What did she like to think? She was having a dumb day and wanted to blame the fog.

Maybe he falls, he slides, if that is a useful word, from his experience of an objective world, the deepest description of space-time, where he does not feel a sense of future direction—he slides into her experience, everyone's, the standard sun-kissed chronology of events.

Am I the first human to abduct an alien?

The fog was somber and bronzed low-rolling toward the coast but then lost form on landfall, taking everything with it in amoebic murk.

If there is no sequential order except for what we engender to make us safe in the world, then maybe it is possible, what, to cross from one nameless state to another, except that it clearly isn't.

She reminded herself she needed batteries. She told herself remember.

It was the kind of day in which you forget words and drop things and wonder what it is you came into the room to get because you are standing here for a reason and you have to tell yourself it is just a question of sooner or later before you remember because you always remember once you are here.

The thing is communicated somehow.

She wax-stripped hair from her armpits and legs. It came ripping off in cold sizzles. She had an acid exfoliating cream, hard-core, prescribed, and after she stripped the hair she rubbed in the cream to remove wastepapery skin in flakes and scales and little rolling boluses that she liked to hold between her fingers and imagine, unmorbidly, as the cell death of something inside her.

She used a monkey-hair brush on her elbows and knees. She wanted it to hurt.

She didn't have to go to Tangier to buy loofahs and orange sticks. It was all in the malls, in the high aisles, and so were the facial brushes, razors and oatmeal scrubs. This was her work, to disappear from all her former venues of aspect and bearing and to become a blankness, a body slate erased of every past resemblance.

She had a fade cream she applied just about everywhere, to depigment herself. She cut off some, then more of the hair on her head. It was crude work that became nearly brutal when she bleached out the color. In the mirror she wanted to see someone who is classically unseen, the person you are trained to look through, bled of familiar effect, a spook in the night static of every public toilet.

She used astringents to remove soap residues, greases and chronic lurking dirt. There were plastic strips that she stuck on and peeled off, grubbing up numerous pluglike impurities from her follicles and pores.

A hidden system, interesting, these tallowy secretions, glandular events of the body cosmos, small festers and eruptions, impacted fats, oils, salt and sweat, and how nearly scholarly the pleasures of extraction.

She found the muscle rub she'd bought for Rey just before he left and she used it just to use it.

She stood looking at him, two bodies in a room. He seemed to recede under observation, inwardly withdraw, not in discomfort, she thought, but spontaneously, autonomically, guided by some law of his body's own devising. She put her hands on his shoulders and looked into his eyes. She thought, When did people start looking into each other's eyes? This is what she did, searchingly, standing in the kitchen with Mr. Tuttle.

Don't touch it. I'll clean it up later.

His eyes were gray but what did it matter. His eyes were off-gray, they were mild and still and unanxious. She looked. She was always looking. She could not get enough. His eyes were gray gone sallow in this harsh light, slightly yellowish, and there were no stirrings of tremulous self.

She framed his face in her hands, looking into him straight-on. What did it mean, the first time a thinking creature looked deeply into another's eyes? Did it take a hundred thousand years before this happened or was it the first thing they did, transcendingly, the thing that made them higher, made them modern, the gaze that demonstrates we are lonely in our souls?

She said, "Why do I think I'm standing closer to you than you are to me?"

She wasn't trying to be funny. It was true, a paradox

of the spectral sort. Then she tried to be funny, using sweet talk and pet names, but soon felt foolish and stopped.

He ate breakfast, or didn't, leaving most of it. Then he stood in the doorway between the kitchen and the long hall that led to the foyer. She sat at the table, waiting. He looked past her or through her and she almost knew what was coming.

He said, "But where are you going?"

He said, "Just a little while into town."

He said, "But there's nothing we need. And I'll get it if we need it. I know what to get. We need some what's-it-called. Scouring powder."

He said, "What?"

She knew almost at once, even before he spoke. She didn't know specifically but sensed and felt the change in him. The tea was smoking in her mug. She sat at the table and watched him and then she knew completely in the first electric exchange because the voice, the voices were not his.

"But we don't need it now this minute. I'll get it when I go. Ajax. That's the stuff. There's nothing to scour right now."

She listened and it was her. Who the hell else. These things she'd said.

"Ajax, son of Telamon, I think, if my Trojan War is still intact, and maybe we need a newspaper because the old one's pretty stale, and great brave warrior, and spear-thrower of mighty distances, and toilet cleanser too."

Do you recognize what you said weeks earlier, and yes, if it is recited back to you, and yes, if it is the last thing you said, among the last things, to someone you loved and would never see again. This is what she'd said to him before he got in the car and drove, if only she'd known, all the way to New York.

"Just for a drive. This is all. I'll take the Toyota," he said, he said, "if I ever find my keys."

This is what the man was saying in the doorway, looking small and weak, beat down by something. It did not seem an act of memory. It was Rey's voice all right, it was her husband's tonal soul, but she didn't think the man was remembering. It is happening now. This is what she thought. She watched him struggle in his utterance and thought it was happening, somehow, now, in his frame, in his fracted time, and he is only reporting, helplessly, what they say.

He said, "Take a walk why don't you. Great day. Leave the car, leave the keys."

He said, "They're in the car. Of course. The keys. Where else? This is it. How can I tell you? This is always it."

He stood in the doorway, blinking. Rey is alive now in this man's mind, in his mouth and body and cock. Her skin was electric. She saw herself, she sees herself crawling toward him. The image is there in front of her. She is crawling across the floor and it is nearly real to her. She feels something has separated, softly come unfixed, and she tries to pull him down to the floor with her, stop him, keep him here, or crawls up onto him or into him, dissolving, or only lies prone and sobs unstoppably, being watched by herself from above.

She could smell his liniment on her body, his muscle rub, and then he was all through talking.

# CHAPTER 6

You stand at the table shuffling papers and you drop something. Only you don't know it. It takes a second or two before you know it and even then you know it only as a formless distortion of the teeming space around your body. But once you know you've dropped something, you hear it hit the floor, belatedly. The sound makes its way through an immense web of distances. You hear the thing fall and know what it is at the same time, more or less, and it's a paperclip. You know this from the sound it makes when it hits the floor and from the retrieved memory of the drop itself, the thing falling from your hand or slipping off the edge of the page to which it was clipped. It slipped off the edge of the page. Now that you know you dropped it, you remember how it happened, or half remember, or sort of see it maybe, or something else. The paperclip hits the floor with an end-to-end bounce, faint and weightless, a sound for which there is no imitative word, the sound of a paperclip falling, but when you bend to pick it up, it isn't there.

That night she stood outside his room and listened to him whimper. The sound was a series of weak cries, half cries, dull and uniform, and it had a faint echo, a feedback, and carried a desolation that swept aside words, hers or anyone's.

She didn't know what it meant. Of course she knew. He had no protective surface. He was alone and unable to improvise, make himself up. She went to the bed and sat there, offering touches and calming sounds, softenings of the night.

He was scared. How simple and true. She tried to tend him, numb him to his fear. He was here in the howl of the world. This was the howling face, the stark, the not-as-if of things.

But how could she know this? She could not.

Maybe he was just deranged, unroutinely nuts. Not that it's ever routine. A nutcase who tries to live in other voices.

He lay curled in a thin blanket. She uncovered him and lay on top. You are supposed to offer solace. She kissed his face and neck and rubbed him warm. She put her hand in his shorts and began to breathe with him, to lead him in little breathy moans. This is what you do when they are scared.



• • •

She thought she saw a bird. Out of the corner of her eye she saw something rise past the window, eerie and bird-like but maybe not a bird. She looked and it was a bird, its flight line perfectly vertical, its streaked brown body horizontal, wings calmly stroking, a sparrow, not wind-hovering but generating lift and then instantly gone.

She saw it mostly in retrospect because she didn't know what she was seeing at first and had to re-create the ghostly moment, write it like a line in a piece of fiction, and maybe it wasn't a sparrow at all but a smaller bird, gray and not brown and spotted and not streaked but not as small as a hummingbird, and how would she ever know for sure unless it happened again, and even then, she thought, and even then again.

It isn't true because it can't be true. Rey is not alive in this man's consciousness or in his palpable verb tense, his walking talking continuum.

Nice word. What does it mean?

She thought it meant a continuous thing, a continuous whole, and the only way to distinguish one part from another, this from that, now from then, is by making arbitrary divisions.

This is exactly what he doesn't know how to do.

She was working her body, crouched on the cold floor, smelling herself.

But it can't be true that he drifts from one reality to another, independent of the logic of time. This is not possible. You are made out of time. This is the force that tells you who you are. Close your eyes and feel it. It is time that defines your existence.

But this is the point, that he laps and seeps, somehow, into other reaches of being, other time-lives, and this is an aspect of his bewilderment and pain.

Somehow. The weakest word in the language. And more or less. And maybe. Always maybe. She was always maybeing.

She knelt, body upright and rigid, legs at hip-distance, head back, arms back, pelvis pushed forward.

Let arms drop down.

Dangle right hand over right foot and then left over left.

Everything flows backward from the pelvis.

Place palms on soles, matching hands to feet.

Time is the only narrative that matters. It stretches events and makes it possible for us to suffer and come out of it and see death happen and come out of it. But not for him. He is in another structure, another culture, where time is something like itself, sheer and bare, empty of shelter.

Hold position.

Everything flows from the pelvis backward to the chest and shoulders and arms, to the furious flung-back head.

Hold position, breathing normally, then abnormally.

Repeat.

• • •

The wind started blowing at noon and was still shaking the windows when she walked along the halls five hours later.

The phone was ringing.

In the kitchen he dropped a glass of water and she extended an arm, seeing the speckled wet begin to spread on the plank floor.

The shrill wind made her uneasy, turning her inward, worse in a way than obliterating snow or deposits of ice that bring down power lines.

She built a fire and then walked out of the room and up the stairs, listening to the walls take the wheezy strain.

In the kitchen she said, "Don't touch it."

The best things in this house were the plank floor in the kitchen and the oak balustrade on the staircase. Just saying the words. Thinking the words.

She said, "Don't touch it," and extended an arm, held out a hand to forestall any effort he might make to pick up the pieces. "I'll clean it up later."

There's something about the wind. It strips you of assurances, working into you, continuous, making you feel the hidden thinness of everything around you, all the solid stuff of a hundred undertakings—the barest makeshift flimsy.

She cleaned it up now. She didn't wait for later. There was something in the moment that she needed to keep.

• • •

She picked up the ringing phone and it was Rey's lawyer at the other end. Something about debts. He was in heavy debt. There were obligations and liabilities. He had debts cascading on other debts. This made her feel good. It was Rey all right. She felt a rush of affection even as the news made her think of her own dimming finances. It was the Rey she knew and not some other. She was sure he hadn't been aware of the situation or had considered it so integral to the condition of his life that knowing about it was just another form of not knowing about it. It occupied no more consciousness than a soft cough on a summer's day. There were loans outstanding, accounts in arrears and taxes long overdue. The man recited numbers in a voice that had a government patent. He pointed out the implications, the sinister transits of spousal responsibility. She laughed gaily and wished him luck.

Then he stopped eating. She sat him down at the table and fed him by hand. She urged and teased. He took some food, then less. She tried force-feeding him but he rejected most of it passively, head averted, or took it in and let it dribble out, let it dangle or spew.

She began to eat less herself. She looked at him and didn't want to eat. He ate next to nothing for three days running and she ate little more. It was suitable in a way. It was what she hadn't thought of on her own.

She looked at him. Poor bastard. She watched him with all the intensity of the first moments and hours but there was something in her look that felt different now, a deathly devotion almost.

Sometimes she followed him through the house. She watched him sleep. Mornings on tape, the questions and answers, little lessons and memorizations, all this faded into a daze of stray talk and then more or less agreed-upon silence. She fed him soup while he sat on the toilet once. The days were toneless and droning.

Finally she got in the car and began to drive the back roads, the fire roads, all the places no one goes, and she left the car and walked through fields to the highest point, the knoll or slope, and scanned the area with her hands cupping her face, looking for Mr. Tuttle.

From a long way off what would he look like, walking the way he walked, narrowly, in curved space?

Like someone you could easily miss. Like someone you technically see but don't quite register in the usual interpretive way.

Like a man anonymous to himself.

Like someone you see and then forget you see. Like that, instantly.

She hadn't been able to find binoculars in the house and what was the point anyway. He wasn't anywhere out here. But she scanned for hours from different sites, hands at her temples to block the glare.

How could such a surplus of vulnerability find itself alone in the world?

Because it is made that way. Because it is vulnerable. Because it is alone.

Or you see him upside down, the way the eye sees before the mind intervenes.

She drove back to the house and walked all through it, room to room, one more time. She thought she'd climb the stairs and walk along the hall and go up to the third floor and find him in the small bedroom off the large empty room at the far end of the hall, as she had the first time, sitting on the edge of the bed in his underwear.

But when he wasn't there she knew he wouldn't be, if that makes sense. A few strides before she reached the doorway she knew he wouldn't be and then he wasn't. She'd known it all along.

She was left to wander the halls, missing him. He was gone so completely there was nothing left, not a single clinging breath of presence, but even as the rooms went empty around her, she felt something in her body try to hold him here.

She began to call the institutions, mindful of the irony, and she listened to recorded voices and poked option buttons and sometimes spoke to someone in a made-up voice of middling concern.

She gave herself two days to do this. On the afternoon of the second day she spoke to a director of psychiatric services at a small hospital about an hour south and he told her that a man who roughly matched the general description she'd provided had been admitted, pending tests, the day before.

She did not press for details. She wanted to believe this was him, being cared for and fed, clean and safe and medicated—free, finally, not to suffer.

But why should it be him? He wasn't mental. Why did she think of calling mental hospitals in the first place, just after she'd discovered him? He didn't act crazy, only impaired in matters of articulation and comprehension. Why did she ever think there was something psychotic about him except in the sense that people who threaten our assumptions are always believed to be mad?

But then it could be him.

She had a thing she stuck in her mouth, an edged implement, smallish, plastic, and she pressed it to the back of her tongue and scraped whatever debris might be massed there, a slurry of food, mucus and bacteria.

This was not a defense against the natural works of the body. This was what she did.

She calculated all the plausible requirements. Then she exceeded them. She shattered their practicality. This is what had to be done. It was necessary to alter the visible form, all the way down to the tongue. She was suppressing something, closing off outlets to the self, all the way down to the scourings at the deep end of the tongue, concealed from human view. The mind willed it on the body.

It was necessary because she needed to do it. This is what made it necessary.

His future is not under construction. It is already there, susceptible to entry.

She had it on tape.

She did not want to believe this was the case. It was her future too. It is her future too.

She played the tape a dozen times.

It means your life and death are set in place, just waiting for you to keep the appointments.

She listened to him say, Don't touch it. I'll clean it up later.

It is the thing you know nothing about.

Then she said it herself, some days later. He'd been in there with her. It was her future, not his.

How much myth do we build into our experience of time?

Don't touch it, she said.

He'd known this was going to happen. These were the words she would say. He'd been in there with her.

I'll clean it up later.

She wanted to create her future, not enter a state already shaped to her outline.



Something is happening. It has happened. It will

happen. This is what she believed. There is a story, a flow of consciousness and possibility. The future comes into being.

But not for him.

He hasn't learned the language. There has to be an imaginary point, a nonplace where language intersects with our perceptions of time and space, and he is a stranger at this crossing, without words or bearings.

But what did she know? Nothing. This is the rule of time. It is the thing you know nothing about.

She listened to him say it, on the tape, in a voice that was probably hers.

But she could have made it up, much of it. Not from scratch. But in retrospect, in memory.

But she had it on tape and it was him and he was saying it.

Then she said it herself but so what. So what if she said the same thing in the same words.

Means nothing. People saying the same thing.

She had him on tape, saying it, but she might easily have misremembered what she herself said when he dropped the water glass. Might have been different. Slightly, very, moderately different.

But so what if it's the same.

Past, present and future are not amenities of language. Time unfolds into the seams of being. It passes through you, making and shaping.

But not if you are him.

This is a man who remembers the future.

Don't touch it. I'll clean it up later.

But if you examine the matter methodically. Be smart, she thought, and analyze coldly. Break it down and scrutinize.

If you examine the matter methodically, you realize that he is a retarded man sadly gifted in certain specialized areas, such as memory retention and mimicry, a man who'd been concealed in a large house, listening.

Nothing else makes sense.

It is the thing no one understands. But it makes and shapes you. And in these nights since he'd left she sometimes sat with a book in her lap, eyes closed, and felt him living somewhere in the dark, and it is colder where he is, it is wintrier there, and she wanted to take him in, try to know him in the spaces where his chaos lurks, in all the soft-cornered rooms and unraveling verbs, the parts of speech where he is meant to locate his existence, and in the material place where Rey lives in him, alive again, word for word, touch for touch, and she opened and closed her eyes and thought in a blink the world had changed.

He violates the limits of the human.

For a while she stopped answering the phone, as she'd done intermittently since the first days back, and when she began to pick it up again, she used another voice.



Her eyes had to adjust to the night sky. She walked

away from the house, out of the spill of electric light, and the sky grew deeper. She watched for a long time and it began to spread and melt and go deeper still, developing strata and magnitudes and light-years in numbers so unapproachable that someone had to invent idiot names to represent the arrays of ones and zeros and powers and dominations because only the bedtime language of childhood can save us from awe and shame.

At first the voice she used on the telephone was nobody's, a generic neutered human, but then she started using his. It was his voice, a dry piping sound, hollow-bodied, like a bird humming on her tongue.

## BODY ART IN EXTREMIS: SLOW, SPARE AND PAINFUL

We are sitting in the dim upper room of an Arab café in Cambridge, Massachusetts, and Lauren Hartke is eating a goat cheese salad, stabbingly, like she's mad at it.

Between bites she talks about the recent performance piece she created in a dungeon space at the Boston Center for the Arts.

She has transformed herself shockingly for this event and although the brief run is over, she continues to look—well, wasted.

She is not pale-skinned so much as colorless, bloodless and ageless. She is rawboned and slightly bug-eyed. Her hair looks terroristic. It is not trimmed but chopped and the natural chestnut luster is ash white now, with faint pink traces.

Can I use the word "albino" and eat lunch in this town again?

"It's vanity. That's all it is," she says. "But vanity is essential to an actor. It's an emptiness. This is where the word comes from. And this is what I work toward and build on."

Hartke, 36, was married to the film director Rey Robles when he committed suicide. Her father, Dr. Robert Hartke, is a classical scholar who is spending his retirement as a field volunteer on archaeological digs in the Aegean. Her late mother, Genevieve Last, was a harpist for the Milwaukee Symphony. She has an older brother, Todd, who is a China specialist in the State Department.

"I don't know if the piece went where I wanted it to go," she is saying. "Some of it is still inside my head, reshaping itself."

The piece, called *Body Time*, sneaked into town for three nights, unadvertised except by word of mouth, and drew eager audiences whose intensity did not always maintain itself for the duration of the show. Hartke clearly wanted her audience to feel time go by, viscerally, even painfully. This is what happened, causing walkouts among the less committed.

They missed the best stuff.

Hartke is a body artist who tries to shake off the body—hers anyway. There is the man who stands in an art gallery while a colleague fires bullets into his arm. This is art. There is the lavishly tattooed man who has himself fitted with a crown of thorns. This is art. Hartke's work is not self-strutting or self-lacerating. She is acting, always in the process of becoming another or exploring some root identity. There is the woman who makes paintings with her vagina. This is art. There are the naked man and woman who charge into each other repeatedly at increasing speeds. This is art, sex and aggression. There is the man in women's bloody underwear who humps a mountain of hamburger meat. This is art, sex, aggression, cultural criticism and truth. There is the man who drives nails into his penis. This is just truth.

Hartke's piece begins with an ancient Japanese woman on a bare stage, gesturing in the stylized manner of Noh drama, and it ends seventy-five minutes later with a naked man, emaciated and aphasic, trying desperately to tell us something.

I saw two of the three performances and I have no idea how Hartke alters her body and voice. She will speak on the subject only in general terms.

"The body has never been my enemy," she says. "I've always felt smart in my body. I taught it to do things other bodies could not. It absorbs me in a disinterested way. I try to analyze and redesign."

(Personal disclosure. Hartke and I are former college classmates who have stayed in pretty regular touch. We used to talk philosophy. I sat in on lectures. She was twisted enough to major in the subject until she dropped out of school to join a troupe of street performers in Seattle.)

Through much of the piece there is sound accompaniment, the anonymous robotic voice of a telephone answering machine delivering a standard announcement. This is played relentlessly and begins to weave itself into the visual texture of the performance.

The voice infiltrates the middle section in particular. Here is a woman in executive attire, carrying a briefcase, who checks the time on her wristwatch and tries to hail a taxi. She glides rather formally (perhaps inspired by the elderly Japanese) from one action to the other. She does this many times, countless times. Then she does it again, half-pirouetting in very slow motion. You may find yourself looking and listening in hypnotic fascination, feeling physically and mentally suspended, or you may cast a glance at your own watch and go slouching down the aisle and into the night.

Hartke says, "I know there are people who think the piece was too slow and repetitious, I guess, and uneventful. But it's probably too eventful. I put too much into it. It ought to be sparer, even slower than it is, even longer than it is. It ought to be three fucking hours."

"Why not four? Why not seven?"

"Why not eight?" she says.

I ask her about the video that runs through the piece, projected onto the back wall. It simply shows a two-lane highway, with sparse traffic. A car goes one way, a car goes the other. There's a slot with a digital display that records the time.

"Something about past and future," she says. "What we can know and what we can't."

"But here we know them both."

"We know them both. We see them both," she says, and that's all she says.

I sit and wait. I nibble at my baba ghanouj. I look at Hartke. What *is* baba ghanouj?

"Maybe the idea is to think of time differently," she says after a while. "Stop time, or stretch it out, or open it up. Make a still life that's living, not painted. When time stops, so do we. We don't stop, we become stripped down, less self-assured. I don't know. In dreams or high fevers or doped up or depressed. Doesn't time slow down or seem to stop? What's left? Who's left?"

The last of her bodies, the naked man, is stripped of recognizable language and culture. He moves in a curious manner, as if in a dark room, only more slowly and gesturally. He wants to tell us something. His voice is audible, intermittently, on tape, and Hartke lip-syncs the words.

Have I ever looked at a figure on a stage and seen someone so alone?

His words amount to a monologue without a context. Verbs and pronouns scatter in the air and then something startling happens. The body jumps into another level. In a series of electro-convulsive motions, the body flails out of control, whipping and spinning appallingly. Hartke makes her body do things I've only seen in animated cartoons. It is a seizure that apparently flies the man out of one reality and into another.

The piece is ready to end.

I take a deep breath and ask the question I don't want to ask. It concerns Rey Robles, their brief marriage and the shock of his suicide.

She looks right through me. I persist, miserably, reminding her of the one time we spent together, the three of us, in Rome, when Rey showed up for dinner with a stray cat on his shoulder.

The memory enters her eyes and she sags a bit. I want to blame the recording device sitting on the table. It's an ergonomically smart four-inch-long, one-and-a-half-ounce, message-storing digital voice recorder, and this is the devil that makes me do it.

She looks into space.

"How simple it would be if I could say this is a piece that comes directly out of what happened to Rey. But I can't. Be nice if I could say this is the drama of men and women versus death. I want to say that but I can't. It's too small and secluded and complicated and I can't and I can't and I can't."

Then she does something that makes me freeze in my seat. She switches to another voice. It is his voice, the naked man's, spooky as a woodwind in your closet. Not taped but live. Not lip-sync'd but real. It is speaking to me and I search my friend's face but don't quite see her. I'm not sure what she's doing. I can almost believe she is equipped with male genitals, as in the piece, prosthetic of course, and maybe an Ace bandage in flesh-tone to bleep out her breasts, with a sprinkle of chest hair pasted on. Or she has trained her upper body to deflate and her lower body to sprout. Don't put it past her.

She says she is going to the restroom. When a waitress shows up with the check, it occurs to me that I can turn off the voice recorder now.

The power of the piece is Hartke's body. At times she makes femaleness so mysterious and strong that it encompasses both sexes and a number of nameless states. In the past she has inhabited the bodies of adolescents, pentecostal preachers, a one-hundred-and-twenty-year-old woman sustained by yogurt and, most memorably, a pregnant man. Her art in this piece is obscure, slow, difficult and sometimes agonizing. But it is never the grand agony of stately images and sets. It is about you and me. What begins in solitary otherness becomes familiar and even personal. It is about who we are when we are not rehearsing who we are.

I sit and wait for Hartke but she doesn't come back.

Mariella Chapman

## CHAPTER 7

The dead squirrel you see in the driveway, dead and decapitated, turns out to be a strip of curled burlap, but you look at it, you walk past it, even so, with a mixed tinge of terror and pity.

Because it was lonely. Because smoke rolled out of the hollows in the wooded hills and the ferns were burnt brown by time. There was a sternness of judgment in the barrens, shades of flamed earth under darkish skies, and in the boulders sea-strewn at the edge of the pine woods, an old stony temper, a rigor of oath-taking and obduracy. And because he'd said what he'd said, that she would be here in the end.

She had a grubby sweater, a pullover, that she put on, accidentally, backward, and then she stood there deciding whether to take it off and put it on again or to feel the slight discomfort of the neck of the sweater riding too high on her own neck. It was a crewneck, a pullover.

She felt the label scratchy at her throat. Not scratchy but something else and she slipped her index and middle fingers inside the neck, elbows thrust up and out, thinking into the blankness of her decision.

They said grim winter grim.

But she is here again, in the house, as he'd said she would be, beyond the limits of the lease agreement. Not that she recalls his exact words. But this is what she'd understood him to say, or his inexact words, or his clear or hazy meaning. She has extended the lease, in whatever words he'd used, and she knows she has taken this action to fulfill the truth of his remark, which probably invalidates whatever truth there may have been. It is not circumstance that has kept her here, or startled chance, but only the remark itself, which she barely recalls him making.

She threw off the sweater and hit her hand on the hanging lamp, which she always forgot was there, and then pulled the sweater down over her head, front side front, as they'd intended in Taiwan.

She knew it was five-thirty and looked at her watch. That's what it was.

When she could not remember what he looked like, she leaned into a mirror and there he was, not really, only hintingly, barely at all, but there in a way, in a manner of thinking, in some mirrors more than others, more than rueful reproduction, depending on the hour and the light and the quality of the glass, the strategies of the glass, with its reversal of left and right, this room or that, because every image in every mirror is only virtual, even when you expect to see yourself.

She climbed the stairs, touching the top of the newel when she reached the landing. This was something she always did because she had to, feeling the oak grain, the carved spurs and ruts in the wood. The post was tapered to an acanthus pattern and was the best thing in the house, just about, along with the plank floor in the kitchen.

She looked at Kotka, after dinner, in Finland.

For five straight days she drove out to the point, the headland, because the standing gulls that look a little dumpy on stilt legs become in their flight the slant carriers of all this rockbound time, taking it out of geology, out of science and mind, and giving it soar and loft and body, bringing it into their flight muscles and bloodflow, into their sturdy hammering hearts, their metronomic hearts, and because she knew this was the day it would happen.

She listened to the sound the wax paper made, advancing along the notched edge of the box when she tore the paper from the roll.

The radiators began to clang, a common occurrence now.

She sat down to eat the food on the plate and thought I'm not hungry. The phone was ringing. She thought in words sometimes, outright and fully formed. She wasn't sure when this began to happen, a day or a month ago, because it seemed to have been the case forever.

Maybe she believed she could deliver herself into his reality, working out the logistics of word and thought, which is how he'd seemed to make his way through a statement or a room.

Maybe there are times when we slide into another reality but can't remember it, can't concede the truth of it because this would be too devastating to absorb.

This is what would happen. She played it through to a certain point, mentally, in the rooms and halls, and then it stopped.

She walked down the fire road past the ramshackle house with the freshly painted white cross rising from the point of the A-frame and the SAVED sign out front.

She cleaned the bathroom, using the spray-gun bottle of disinfectant. Then she held the nozzle of the spray gun to her head, seeing herself as doing what anyone might do, alone, without special reference to the person's circumstances. It was the pine-scent bottle, the pistol-grip bottle of tile-and-grout cleaner, killer of mildew, and she held the nozzle, the muzzle to her head, finger pressed to the plastic trigger, with her tongue hanging out for effect.

This is what people do, she thought, alone in their lives.

She was happy in a way, in many ways, folded in hope, having the house to come back to after long mornings rambling in stands of jack pine and spruce, where she named bog plants for him, spelling out the words, or whole afternoons when she crouched on the massive granite slabs out at the point, the promontory, and watched the weather build and the plumes of booming surf shoot higher, because this is what would happen when she returned, running her hand over shags of sea moss and knowing she would mount the stairs, touching the top of the newel at the landing, and walk down the hall into his time.

The stories she told herself did not seem hers exactly. She was in them so heedlessly they seemed to come from a deeper source, whatever that might mean, a thing that was overtaking her. Where did they come from? They did not come from the newspaper. She hadn't read a paper in some time. She looked at a paper in town, at the general store, front page only, and it seemed to be another framework altogether, a slick hysteria of picture and ink, the world so fleetingly easy to love and hate, so reliable and forgettable in its recipes and wars and typographical errors.

When she walked out of the store, she saw the Japanese woman coming toward her, the white-haired woman, and she wore a padded jacket and had her hands concealed. Her hands were fisted up inside the sleeves of her jacket, for warmth, and she watched the woman, sleeves seemingly empty, and cursed herself for not having thought of this for the piece, because it was fantastic, no hands, it was everything she needed to know about the woman and would have been perfect for the piece, inexplicably missing hands, and she tortured herself with the mystery of a gesturing figure, half lit, no hands, and smiled falsely at the woman when she passed.

Why not sink into it? Let death bring you down. Give death its sway.

Why shouldn't the death of a person you love bring you into lurid ruin? You don't know how to love the ones you love until they disappear abruptly. Then you understand how thinly distanced from their suffering, how sparing of self you often were, only rarely unguarded of heart, working your networks of give-and-take.

She held these ideas every way she was. Eyes, mind and body. She moved about the town's sloping streets unnoticed, holding these ideas, buying groceries and hardware and playing through these thoughts to a certain point, in the long hall, among the locks, tools and glassware.

Why shouldn't his death bring you into some total scandal of garment-rending grief? Why should you accommodate his death? Or surrender to it in thin-lipped tasteful bereavement? Why give him up if you can walk along the hall and find a way to place him within reach?

Sink lower, she thought. Let it bring you down. Go where it takes you.



Sometimes she thought in these motive forms,

addressing someone who wasn't quite her, and other times in other ways. She thought in faces, there in the air, the little missing man's when she could recall it, just outside the bony sockets of her eyes.

I am Lauren. But less and less.

When she got out of the car, someone was there. She wasn't out of the car, she was still half in, beginning to unbend, and a figure loomed above her in the driveway.

She nearly fell back into the seat. It was a jolting moment. She looked up at him, a large man, middle-aged, talking to her.

When she rose to full height, she was able to glimpse his car, parked at the side of the house. She listened to him. She tried to listen to what he was saying and to read the situation, fix its limits accurately.

"Assure you I don't mean to intrude. Tried calling several times. No answer. I understand completely. You're here to get away from that."

"And you're here?"

She was angry now. The looming effect, the menace began to fade. The fear began to melt back into her body, into the bloodstream and nerve fibers, the ridges of her fingertips, and she shut the car door hard, she swung the door shut.

"To talk about the house," he said in a tone of some detachment. "It seems this is my house, still. My wife's and mine."

He stepped back and eased around to look at the

house, bringing it materially into the dialogue—his house. Now that he'd looked, there could be no doubt.

"And there is something you want to discuss."

"Yes exactly," he said and seemed to burst into a kind of pinkness, pleased by her grasp of the moment.

There was a pause. The man had a slightly edgeworn air, a malaise perhaps shaped over many years.

She said, "Who invites who in?"

He put up his hands.

"Not necessary. Wouldn't think. No, no, absolutely."

Then he laughed at her remark. It hit him finally and he laughed, showing sepia teeth. She waited. She was getting interested in this. She began to feel she was fitting into something, becoming comfortable out here, in the driveway, with the owner of the house.

"Has it been satisfactory then?"

"Mostly, I think, yes."

"Because if there's anything."

"No, it's fine, I think. Rooms."

"Yes."

"Rooms and rooms."

It was cold. She wondered if it was supposed to be so cold.

"Yes," he said. "Been in the family. Let's see, forever. But the upkeep."

"I would imagine."

"The work, the attention. We have a history of large families, I'm afraid. The endless sort of, you know, repairing, repainting. Something always needs attending to."

She waited for him to mention Alma in this regard, his wife, and the fact that the children were grown and living elsewhere now.

"And what we were hoping in fact."

His body stretched, it strained upward and askant in a little epiphany of bright expectation. She saw him in this gesture as a man trying to unsnarl himself from a lifetime's shyness and constriction.

"Is that you wouldn't mind."

She listened, practically seeing the words, and liked him a bit more, and felt an easy alertness, a sense of being inside the moment.

"Yes."

"You see there's a chest of drawers. It's stored in a room somewhere upstairs. Wrapped, I think. Probably wrapped in that padded fabric they use. Maybe you've come across it. Because it was about to be moved, shipped, and then somehow, well, you know how these things don't always happen when they're supposed to. It's a delicate piece, in two parts, and fairly old."

This is not what he was supposed to say.

"One of the unused rooms on the top floor, wrapped in quilts. And what we'd like to do," he said.

She noted the tracery of blood vessels in his face, a large man, yes, and getting on, getting old, his skin beginning to stretch, eyelines deepening, and he was supposed to say something about Mr. Tuttle, why he'd left and where he'd gone and whatever else there was to say about the man, to clear up, to explain and analyze.

"Is, if we sent someone to get it, perhaps you wouldn't mind the inconvenience. We've tried calling and the woman has called, the real estate person. It's an old family piece. We thought we'd like to have it refinished and placed in our bedroom, at home. We've talked about it for some time. Current home, of course. But what with one thing and another."

He was afraid to stop talking because she'd given no indication either way and seemed to be disengaging herself from the scene. He stepped back and executed another half turn and they stood there in the cold, the owner and the tenant in the driveway, looking vaguely at the house.

She tried to remember what he looked like and then forgot his name. But briefly. It was only brief and it wasn't his name. It was her name that she'd given him.

In the morning she heard the noise.

She knew it was seven-twenty, just about, and looked at the kitchen clock. That's what it was.

She understood at once that this was not the noise from the third floor. It was different, not so high in the structure of the house, less furtive than before.

She stepped slowly through the rooms, knowing it would happen like this, as chant, a man's chanted voice, his, and it paced her way up the stairs and measured the flex of her hand on the newel. Being here has come to me. Because it was lonely, the coast in this season, and because she had to touch the newel every time.

She moved past the landing and turned into the hall, feeling whatever she felt, exposed, open, something you could call unlayered maybe, if that means anything, and she was aware of the world in every step.

She knew how it would happen, driving the car past the NEW USED signs, with firewood stacked in every lean-to and shrouded in blue tarp outside garages and barns. She'd return to the house and mount the stairs, past U-HAUL and AUTO PARTS, and walk along the hall on the second floor, in chanted motion, fitting herself to a body in the process of becoming hers.

She could hear him in her chest and throat, speaking hypnotically, and she approached the door to her room, the bedroom, not so high in the structure of the house. The room upstairs had nothing in it but a dresser wrapped in moving men's quilts. His time was here, his measure or dimension or whatever labored phrase you thought to call it.

She was a thousand times a fool. She moved toward the door and was a fool this way and that but not in her room, driving past AUTO BODY and NEW USED, with firewood stacked in canvas and sailcloth, because that's where Rey was intact, in his real body, smoke in his hair and clothes.

She knew how it would happen, past the point of playing it through, because she refused to yield to the limits of belief.

Once she steps into the room, she will already have been there, now, at night, getting undressed. It is a question of fitting herself to the moment, throwing off a grubby sweater, her back to the bed. She stands barefoot, raising her arm out of the sweater and striking a hand on something above. She remembers the hanging lamp, totally wrong for the room, metal shade wobbling, and then turns and looks, knowing what she will see.

He sits on the edge of the bed in his underwear, lighting the last cigarette of the day.

Are you unable to imagine such a thing even when you see it?

Is the thing that's happening so far outside experience that you're forced to make excuses for it, or give it the petty credentials of some misperception?

Is reality too powerful for you?

Take the risk. Believe what you see and hear. It's the pulse of every secret intimation you've ever felt around the edges of your life.

They are two real bodies in a room. This is how she feels them, in the slivered heart of the half second it takes to edge around the doorpost, with hands that touch and rub and mouths that open slowly. His cock is rising in her slack pink fist. Their mouths are ajar for tongues, nipples, fingers, whatever projections of flesh, and for whispers of was and is, and their eyes come open into the soul of the other.

She stopped at the edge of the doorway, aware of the look on her face.

They will already have slept and wakened and gone down to breakfast, where they muddle through their separate routines, pouring the milk and shaking the juice, a blue jay watching from the feeder, and she sniffs the granules in the soya box. It is the simplest thing in the world when she goes out to his car and takes his car keys and hides them, hammers them, beats them, eats them, buries them in the bone soil on a strong bright day in late summer, after a roaring storm.

But before she stepped into the room, she could feel the look on her face. She knew this look, a frieze of false anticipation.

She stood a while, thinking into this. She stopped at room's edge, facing back into the hall, and felt the emptiness around her. That's when she rocked down to the floor, backed against the doorpost. She went twistingly down, slowly, almost thoughtfully, and opened her mouth, *oh,* in a moan that remained unsounded. She sat on the floor outside her room. Her face still wore a decorative band, a trace across the eyes of the prospect of wonders. It was a look that nearly floated free of her so she could puff her cheeks, childlike, and blow it away.

She thought she would not bother looking in there. It was pathetic to look. The room faced east and would be roiled in morning light, in webby sediment and streams of sunlit dust and in the word *motes*, which her mother liked to use.

Maybe it was all an erotic reverie. The whole thing was a city built for a dirty thought. She was a sexual hysteric, ha. Not that she believed it.

She sat there, thinking into the blankness of her decision. Then she worked herself up along the doorpost, slowly, breathing completely, her back to the fluted wood, squat-rising, drawing out the act over an extended length of time. Her mother died when she was nine. It wasn't her fault. It had nothing to do with her.

The room was empty when she looked. No one was there. The light was so vibrant she could see the true colors of the walls and floor. She'd never seen the walls before. The bed was empty. She'd known it was empty all along but was only catching up. She looked at the sheet and blanket swirled on her side of the bed, which was the only side in use.

She walked into the room and went to the window. She opened it. She threw the window open. She didn't know why she did this. Then she knew. She wanted to feel the sea tang on her face and the flow of time in her body, to tell her who she was.

## About the Author

DON DELILLO published his first short story when he was twenty-three. He has since published twelve novels and two stage plays. He was awarded the Jerusalem Prize in 1999, the first American to be so honored. His novel *White Noise* won the National Book Award; *Libra* won the Irish *Times* International Fiction Prize; *Mao II* won the PEN/Faulkner Award for Fiction. His last novel, *Underworld,* won the Howells Medal of the American Academy of Arts and Letters for the most distinguished work of fiction of the past five years.